Nasty, Brutish, and Short

Lessons and Laughs from an Overseas Officer

Todd Millick

Hamilton Books

An Imprint of
Rowman & Littlefield
Lanham • Boulder • New York • Toronto • Plymouth, UK

Library of Congress Control Number: 2016936247
ISBN: 978-0-7618-6782-1 (pbk : alk. paper)—ISBN: 978-0-7618-6783-8 (electronic)

All statements of fact, opinion, or analysis expressed are those of the author and do not reflect the official positions or views of the U.S. Government. Nothing in the contents should be construed as asserting or implying U.S. Government authentication of information or endorsement of the author's views. This material has been reviewed solely for classification.

To my Mom and Dad

Contents

Preface

I don't pretend to be an intellectual or a philosopher. I just look.
—Josef Koudelka

Convention dictates that books have a Preface. Convention doesn't think that you, dear reader, are qualified to jump right into the text. You need to be taken by the hand and presented with a sturdy context to start the journey. Maybe even told upfront what the book's about. Because, otherwise, you'd never get the full meaning. Or, god forbid, you'd wait until the last chapter to form an opinion. Send your complaints to the people at Convention.

This Preface is rather short, mostly because there's not much to get in the book. What you see is what you get. And, like a little kid, I just want to start the trip already. The book, as you can see, is a collection of essays about faraway places. These are lands you may never visit but have wondered what their personalities were like, and what it was like to live there.

This is no "Day in the Life of an Overseas Officer." The countries are the protagonists in the story. And in order to present the most accurate impressions, I try to let them speak for themselves. So their pasts, and presents, are the real prelude. And they said a lot to me over the past twenty years.

What they said is that life overseas is nothing like how it's portrayed on the news or in the movies. To me, it's not even close to what was taught in school. In all of these cases, the storyteller's agenda usually involves some kind of moral or maxim. But when the countries are left to narrate themselves, they often tell different stories—ones that, as the title suggests, may not have a heroine or a happy ending. And the book follows their lead by not force-feeding emotions or conclusions. But it does attempt to place the countries into everyday contexts that help the reader relate to them more easily. And, hopefully, laugh a little at the same time, like I learned to do.

This is also no deep treatise on international relations or how to survive a hostage crisis. Instead, its philosophy is that life, even in the most violent and depressing places, is often ridiculous—sometimes tragically, most of the time, comically. As a result, it should be savored as much as possible but not over-analyzed. It should be a funny, not a brooding, experience. But then, dear reader, you would've figured this out by the end.

Your guide on this journey around the world is well-qualified. I spent nearly the last twenty years—the second half of my life— overseas in the United States government. And, half of that time, I was fortunate to be on the front lines of history. Bluntly put, much of what happened around me could have been made into a movie. But, because few cameras were rolling, I chose to write this book.

I was in Algeria during the Civil War, in Pakistan before and after 9/11, in Iraq after the 2003 invasion. I witnessed Afghanistan hold its first two national elections and Egypt ignite a revolution. I watched Serbia react to Milosevic's death and Montenegro celebrate its independence from Yugoslavia.

Along the way, I have been kicked, cursed, bitten, robbed, spit on, poisoned, tear gassed, mortared, rocketed, and slapped—by women—on four continents. All while having the time of my life.

There is one word of caution. I believe that, if some of these stories upset you and your moral compass, your beef resides more with reality, something in which I played only a minor role, than with the characterizations of the people or places. Indeed, if you're still thinking about the book after you put it down and not, at least, smiling, it had the wrong effect.

As they say, "Life," like this book, "is a journey." I wish you a pleasant trip.

Chapter One

Looking Backward

Bulgaria

The historian looks backward. In the end he also believes back-ward.
—Friedrich Nietzsche

An expatriate falls hardest for the first country.

It is your first and only true love. The place that future countries will be measured against. The one who will make up for past wrongs. Who will make your life whole again. Because after all, if there were nothing missing, you wouldn't have left home in the first place.

We choose a country the way we choose a mate. We look for qualities that we idealize, along with those missing in ourselves. And we consider a variety of different traits when making this selection. Let's face it, there are so many countries to choose from, so many fish in the sea. There might as well be an "eHarmony" app for picking your dream land.

For example, do you want a rich or poor country?

Are you looking for a nice place that's going to be comfortable and take good care of you?

Or do you want an adventure, a project, someplace where you can get your hands dirty?

Are you superficial? Do you care if the country is good-looking—I mean, beautiful? Or are you okay with lepers in the streets?

Are you open to different races and religions? Or do you want to stick to what's familiar?

Are you somewhat self-loathing? In other words, do you want an anti-American country? One who will spit in your face and say you've been bad?

Even before you meet her, you are eager to understand your new country—her past, her problems, her hopes and dreams. You study her language because you've been told that communication is the key to a strong relationship.

You want to know her. To love her.

And you want her to accept you. Even love you back.

Then you move there. You travel thousands of miles, across land and ocean, to meet your one true love for the first time ever.

And she has a giant wart on her nose.

But you don't care. You romanticize her features and paint over her flaws. You compare her to others' loves and boast how much better yours is.

You will defend her, even her shortcomings, to the death. It doesn't matter how poor, ugly, or rat-infested. I know a guy who swears Burkina Faso is the greatest place on Earth. Burkina Faso.

Anyway, it's probably just a beauty mark.

Where else would a lack of basic necessities be described as "charming" or "exotic?" If the following things happened back home, it would be chaos. There would be riots in the streets.

For example, there's no bread in the shops. "Eh," you reckon, "eating is over-rated."

There's no hot water. "Cold showers build character."

They beat their women. "You can't impose Western values on every country around the world!"

In the end, you conclude there must be something wrong with you, if you continue to find their ways strange. "It's not you, it's me!" you declare.

But you also secretly plan to have that "beauty mark" removed the first chance you get.

Indeed, eventually, you try to change her. Slowly at first. Then, after realizing that nothing has changed, you become more desperate. "What's the problem?" you ask yourself. "She can't possibly be happy living like this. She must want to change."

In the end, you're right, she's probably not happy. But she's been this way for millennia, and one lone American coming for a year or two will not make her change, no matter how many times you've read *Three Cups of Tea*. This is the way things have always been done.

Some fall so hard for their countries, they believe theirs is unique, that they'll never meet another one like it. So they "marry" it and stay forever. They go native, surrendering much of themselves and their own culture to be one with their true love. You've seen these people when they return for a visit to the US. They wear the local garb of their country, talk endlessly about it, try to get others to try its dishes.

Bulgaria was my first love.

In the early 1990s, Eastern Europe was the new frontier. Communism had ended. The "Wall" had come down. Americans poured into Poland and Hungary, starting rock bands and teaching English. Prague was the new Paris for the latest "restless generation." The US had won the Cold War, and we were celebrities. Americans were greeted like the Allied armies that liberated Europe fifty years earlier. Young East Europeans couldn't get enough of Western culture. And we were the messengers.

For many, this was their first experience as expats. It changed them forever.

Moving almost anywhere overseas is the fastest way for a young middle-class American to live like a rich man. It is an instant ticket to wealth and fame, without any of the hard work or ingenuity. And it's all just a plane ride away.

When you get there, for example, most things are cheap, so any money you have—especially dollars—makes you, at least, seem rich.

As an American, you often get immediate respect and admiration, whether you deserve it or not. You are the representative for all power and prosperity that comes from the US.

Most foreigners want your life, your things, to be like you. Such celebrity status is intoxicating, addictive. It's one of the reasons why they say, "Once an expat, always an expat."

By the mid-1990s, Central Europe became settled, even overrun, with tourists. Prague became expensive and cliché. Its day was over. The frontier was closed.

Rolling Stone declared, "Go (farther) east, young man!"

Or southeast, more specifically, to the Balkans. To southeast Europe and Bulgaria.

To most at the time, Bulgaria seemed like a scary place—poor, cold, and dark. It was near the bottom of the list of "Most Happy Countries."

Bulgaria was moving in the complete opposite direction of its neighbors. Instead of celebrating the end of the communists, its people had voted them back in. And, with them, the "Good old bad days."

"Unhappy days are here again!" they seemed to sing.

The electricity went out. Shops ran out of food. Hot water was a luxury. Workers made fifty bucks a month, if they had a job. The mafia—or rather, *"biznesmen"*—had taken over the economy, and crime resembled 1920s Chicago.

And, as my mom pointed out, "Gypsies live there!"

I couldn't wait to get there.

Bulgaria was the "Wild, Wild East." A prairie for outlaws and adventurers. It was raw and beautiful. Dark, blank, and wide open. A place to write your name on the wall with unique and meaningful experiences. A secret world where time seemed to stand still. To me, the country was filled with magic and mystery.

I moved to Bulgaria to live in the past.

After studying history for years, I wanted to see it up close— taste it, smell it, feel it. I wanted to look backward, to experience the old ways that had disappeared, that only existed in books. What better way than to move to a place where history had not ended?

I could tell it was the past simply by looking around me— nothing had changed in decades. Everything, everywhere, was old. And not merely old but outdated and obsolete. I imagined it was still the 1950s or 1960s. The same cars, roads, buildings—and ideas.

I also wanted to live in a world that was simple and slow, where you could recognize the human in a fellow being. Where you were not too busy to see beauty around you. Where the moment, the here and now, was all that mattered. A place where people lived by different ways and means.

Clearly, some of these ways were forced on Bulgaria by a lack of means. Others, I imagined, were conscious decisions made by a people who rejected more modern ways.

The country was different from my world. You could feel it on the street. You could smell it in the air. Expats like to say that you can just "smell it" when a place has lots of "culture." And you could smell lots of things in Bulgaria.

It was easy to fall for Bulgaria. For me, it was love at first sight.

I've always gone for the underdogs, the simple, almost-but-not-quite-pretty ones who stayed in the back at school dances. Not those who were loud or pretentious.

A local summed up his country in one short sentence—"Bulgarians are poor but beautiful." That was the only tagline I needed to hear.

Such a country would be my new home.

The day I arrived in Bulgaria, my watch stopped working. It was a good omen.

In the 1990s, the capital, Sofia, was a great place for Americans for prosaic reasons. Teaching jobs were plentiful, since Bulgarians wanted to learn English and few native speakers made it to that corner of Europe.

The first year, I taught at a local university. The next, I researched at the Academy of Sciences.

The most rewarding part was time with young Bulgarians. With all the dramatic changes in Eastern Europe, they were caught in the middle, pulled in two directions. For their parents, communism, despite its reputation, had been, largely, a good thing. It had allowed a relatively small and poor country to industrialize quickly, to make up for centuries of lost time. As a result, many of these parents had voted for its return.

But the young wanted to live like the West. They were captivated by Western movies, music, and lifestyle. Such a lifestyle offered the complete opposite of their cold, gray apartment blocks and all they wanted to do was join in on the fun, far away from their Eastern abodes. Most, however, couldn't get visas, even if by some miracle they'd had the money to travel.

Some took jobs to save for plane tickets. An old friend of mine worked as a waitress at "Eddy's Pub," owned by a shady Canadian with the same name. One night, Eddy told my friend to get him a "Sprite." She didn't understand, asked him to repeat himself. So he yelled, less politely, "I said, get me a goddamn Sprite!" Shaken by his temper, she ran to the kitchen and searched frantically through the stacks of sodas. Another waiter asked her what she was looking for. "Ivan!" she exclaimed. "Which ones are the goddamn Sprites?"

There were relatively few full-time Americans in Bulgaria at the time—maybe less than a hundred. When I spoke English on a bus, others stared with astonished looks—wide-eyed, open-mouthed, as if an alien had been teleported to their planet.

This was out of the ordinary, however, because Bulgarians are normally stoic people. They consider smiling, or any emotion, really, a sign of weakness, even stupidity. As a result, it's hard to tell when someone likes you. After breaking down barriers—and by this I mean, of course, consuming large amounts of alcohol—a few of them started to open up.

And I found that they really like Americans. Or, at least, they'd really like to be like Americans. But while they're waiting for that, the next best thing would be to hang out with me.

So Americans didn't lack for attention or dates. As the married man who sold me falafel sandwiches said, "In Bulgaria, you're not a real man if you don't have at least three girlfriends."

A friend called the whole experience the "Commie-sutra."

It took years for my ego to return to normal.

Still, I tried to reciprocate. I submersed myself, body and soul, into Bulgaria and its culture. I learned its language, read its poets, studied its history, heard Bulgarians sing at jazz clubs and the opera, explored every corner of the country, and walked every inch of the city.

I was young and wifeless and carefree. I could do almost anything I wanted.

I was a kid on a two-year recess, living in a giant playground.

I wrote and drank late each night. I slept till noon and played with stray dogs.

I became a reflection of the country. And why not? At the time, we wanted the same things out of life. We both hated growing up and had no idea what we'd do when we got there. We were a perfect match.

I met a thousand different people from every level of society—hobos to the nouveau riche, students to government ministers.

All I learned and idealized at University, I put into practice in Bulgaria—socially, musically, scholarly, historically, and alcoholically. "I drink, therefore I am!" I declared.

Meanwhile, the country around me was falling apart. Many stores were empty, the local currency, collapsing. Inflation spiraled out of control. There were food, water, gas, and electricity shortages. The mafia extorted money from local businesses and burned them down when they didn't pay. They also killed each other. A favorite method involved throwing another gangster, kicking and screaming, off a high balcony.

Even American friends who lived in Serbia were afraid of the place. When they drove to Greece, they raced through Bulgaria as fast as possible, unwilling to stop for gas or drinks.

For many Bulgarians, life was bleak and hopeless. They deserved better.

Never have so many been so miserable so that so few could be so happy.

And amidst the chaos, I felt like Nero, playing while the city burned—or froze.

As Dickens might have said, "It was the best of times (in) the worst of times."

But isn't that when meaningful events happen? After all, Bogie fell for Bergman when the Nazis were about to overrun Paris. Because let's face it. Very little actually happens in Switzerland.

The severe economic crisis sewed fear and doubt among the population about the future, making it also "The Age of the Present." When you were with someone, you were with them. There were few distractions. You saw more of them and you saw them more clearly. Most believed in acting on impulse. There was an emotional immediacy, since it seemed almost anything could happen and everything could change—usually for the worse—in an instant. As a result, there were no hang-ups, hold-ups, or taboos. Intimate relationships didn't take weeks or months. "Love," for lack of a better word, often happened "at first sight" and was acted upon. And, because there were no gadgets or games, no internet or modern conveniences, most were in no hurry to return home. So Bulgarians "played" outside, using the city as their living room. They sat in cafes for hours at a time—every day—talking with friends or reading newspapers. They stayed out for "one last drink," which seemed to last half the night, walking home at three in the morning.

Most people were the same, good or bad. They had no money, future, place to go, or way to get there. So they stayed put and made the best of it.

People who survived the Great Depression describe similar attitudes at the time, though such ideas seem radical today.

Obviously, it wasn't as bad if you had dollars. Even poor expats could live like kings. Rent an apartment in the center of Sofia for less than a hundred dollars a month. Take a taxi across town for a buck. Buy bread, when available, for a nickel. The opera? Less than a dollar. The electric bill? About three. Booze was cheap enough to make anyone an alcoholic.

Americans turned easily into Bohemians. And being eccentric was often mistaken for being poor, many of us certainly looked poorer than any locals.

Bulgaria was a place to wear your old clothes, sleep late, not shave, drink early and often, and exist for months on bread and cheese.

Once, an American friend, with only a few dollars left at the end of the month, chose to buy a book with his money, rather than pay for electricity, which was promptly shut off. He happily read his new book by candle light.

Me? I lived in a small, scary apartment downtown for seventy-five bucks a month.

I was over-charged.

It was an apartment in name only—nothing worked within the four walls. Even Bulgarians shook their heads when they saw the place.

The kitchen had no appliances, no oven, toaster, or fridge, though it did boast a faucet. I didn't care—I took most of my meals on the outside. Bulgarian food is fresh and simple. The country is called the "Greengrocer of Europe," with plenty of outdoor markets and street food vendors.

I also had no TV or washing machine for two years. The latter, especially, were rare in Bulgaria at the time. Before you shed any crocodile tears, you should try washing your clothes, by hand, for just one week, with no hot water, in the middle of winter. It's cold. Really, really cold. Still, eventually, I got a routine and took a few pieces of clothing with me each week as I shivered in a cold shower.

If anything, the washing machine belongs in an American "You don't know what you've got till it's gone" department. When you finally return to the US, you say a prayer to the "laundry gods," thanking them for The Greatest Invention Ever.

But even if there had been appliances in the kitchen, they would not have gotten much use, due to the frequent brown and blackouts in the city. Sometimes the electricity went out due to capacity problems, while at other times, Gypsies stole neighborhood power lines.

The rest of the apartment wasn't much better. There were mice under the bed and inside the walls. I heard them scurry at night when I turned off the light. The window had a baseball-sized hole into which I stuffed a towel.

The telephone—my only contact with the outside world—was on the fritz most days. In fact, I'd heard a statistic that only a third of local calls in Sofia were routed correctly on the first try. During peak times, you had no shot of calling even across town. Indeed, Bulgaria was one of the few places where you could actually use the excuse that, really, you tried calling, but the phones were out— and she had to believe you.

In the summer, farmers came downtown to cut the grass behind the apartment blocks, by hand, with scythes. This was lawn care, Bulgarian-style. They gathered up the clippings and dumped them in a horse-drawn cart, which was hauled back to the village to feed the animals.

One of the more famous hardships happened in the winter of 1994, when the city shut off the water.

That's not quite fair, they didn't shut it off completely. Rather, the government started a regime in which water was turned off for three days, then back on for one day. God help you if you lived on the top floor, which had such poor water pressure, you were often left, literally, "high and dry." The regime lasted the entire winter.

The theory on the street was that mobbed-up members of the government sold the country's water reserves to Turkey. How they could do this, I have no idea, but it sounded like a good explanation at the time.

Indeed, conspiracy theories are one of the Balkans' main commodities. The population produces them as a sort of "comfort food": easily digested and make you feel good inside. They're also a kind of superstition, helping to explain hardships, especially those that seem beyond your control, while assigning blame to shadowy organizations that secretly control everything, such as "criminal elements" or the "government." Having both of these guys in the same theory was even better.

These theories also serve to soothe when the organizations are "good," because in those cases, they make sure things run as they should. When they're "bad," however, they make life miserable. Either way, the theories help you believe someone is out there watching over things. Unfortunately, I've found that it's not conspiracy theory, but rather chaos theory, that explains most of these kinds of events. Chaos, the opposite of conspiracy, proclaims that, in fact, there's no one out there keeping an "eye on things," that events happen capriciously for reasons such as "There just wasn't enough rain over the summer," or "A huge pipe burst and most of the city's water supplies were lost." But such beliefs would have been disconcerting to the average Bulgarian.

There were also "rumors," or sneak-peaks of possible conspiracy theories. It was like the theories were getting a "trial run" to see if others took to them. One of the rumors at the time whispered that the city was also going to shut off—completely—the already dismal amount of heat provided to apartment blocks (Bulgaria took its communism to an extreme and even centralized the distribution of heat and hot water across the city.). According to some, the measure would lead to a winter "genocide" of the older population. This particular rumor never came true, but the government did raise the price of heat to levels that many could no longer afford.

Residents coped with the water crisis by filling every imaginable container, including their bathtubs—from which water was used to fill up the toilets—with water on the days it was on.

At the end of the first year, when I left my apartment, I simply threw out the sheets and towels. They could've walked out on their own anyway. After all, I hadn't washed them the entire year. Or cleaned the bathroom, floors, or kitchen, for that matter. Not once. With all the water problems, they just were not a priority.

Turns out, all those warnings about germs and bacteria are mostly designed to sell more cleaning products, which you apparently don't need.

Eventually, no matter how much you loved your country, you become disillusioned with her. You grow tired of her little quirks and foibles. They're just not that cute anymore.

And that wart has only grown bigger and bigger.

You begin to question why you are there. Whether it should just be a short-term "project." Maybe, even, if it's all been a waste of time.

The adrenaline starts to wear off. You grow apart. The honeymoon is over.

You pick up a *National Geographic* and start to look at pictures of other countries behind her back.

My awakening came while listening to BBC radio on one of those cold, dark nights. There was a story about education in Vietnam, wherein the reporter was interviewing young students. They were so full of life, so excited just to be learning—maybe just to be alive. They reflected their country—young, energetic, and poor—yet happy.

At this point, I looked around and realized they were the complete opposite of all that surrounded me.

Everything in Bulgaria was old, dour, and depressing—from the clunky Ladas, to the frozen, gray sky; from the rude store clerks, to the old babas selling nuts on the sidewalk.

My perspective had changed. Though Bulgaria was fascinating for a while, eventually the old got old. It crumbled into misery and decay. And living in the past felt the same way. Maybe my soul was ancient, but my body and mind were still young.

I now hated the past. I hated the old.

History, a body of mostly terrible, outdated ideas and ways of life, became my enemy. After all, the past was full of hardship, wars, and massacres. Why would anyone glorify these times? Why wouldn't you try to move forward and improve your life?

The people were hard-headed and refused to change, that's why. They were suspicious of anything new or different. They only wanted the same old things, which were, literally, old things. They looked backward for nearly everything and, in the process, remained backward.

Maybe worst of all were the hoops I had to jump through just to stay in the place. It was like paying to get beaten up.

At that time, Bulgaria let Americans live in the country for only thirty days at a time. And who could blame them? Clearly, millions of us were flocking across its borders to steal work from the poor locals, or to take advantage of the generous welfare programs. Others had eyes on getting that precious Bulgarian citizenship.

So, each month, I traveled to the southern border, got off the bus in Greece, got an entry stamp in my passport, walked back across "no-man's land" into Bulgaria, got stamped again, and waited for the next bus to Sofia to come along. It was a twelve-hour ordeal, door to door. The fresh Bulgarian stamp gave me another thirty day ticket to "The Magic Kingdom." And the look on the border guards' faces as I walked past made the trip entertaining.

And, each month, I asked myself why I was doing all this for a country that clearly didn't want me.

That song, "My Love is Alive," by Gary Wright, began to stick in my head. Only, I sang the lyrics as, "My Love is a Lie."

Eventually, the dream ended, and I finally woke up. It was time to leave.

Simply put, love fades and, when it does, it's best to say "Goodbye."

We had some good times, even some deep, meaningful experiences. But, in the end, we were probably not meant for each other, like an organ transplanted into another body. Sometimes it takes, but most times, it's just too different.

Ultimately, you remember that you're just passing through.

I was not Bulgarian and never would be, no matter how long I lived there. The locals did not understand me, and vice versa. To truly understand someone, you have to be like them—one of their tribe, country, and family. You have to be born and grow up there. The Bulgarians, perhaps a little bitterly, reminded me regularly that all I had to do was buy a plane ticket, take my passport, and leave.

And, in the end, that's what I did. Contrary to what I believed when I first arrived, Bulgaria was not the only one in the world and did not have everything I wanted out of life.

I was very happy to have known such a girl—I mean, country. And I returned to it, regularly, just as I do in this book. But there were so many other things to do—I was about to join the US government. So many other "fish in the ocean." And so much more to see.

Chapter Two

Not a High School Quarterback

Chad

Hell is empty, and all the devils are here.
—William Shakespeare, *The Tempest*

Chad's the first country I've ever been where, until just recently, you were, not only, not required to wear a helmet while riding a motorcycle, but it was actually illegal to wear one. That's right. It's against the law to protect yourself during an accident.

Of course, that wasn't the logic behind the law. It appeared to have its roots in counter-terrorism precautions—the police wanted to make sure you couldn't hide your face, even while riding around town. But come on. How many Chadian criminals are notorious enough to be spotted on the back of a motorcycle? Perhaps the government was more afraid the Chadians would stick out their tongues at the police as they whizzed by.

Update: In 2015, the government in N'djamena passed a new law requiring motorcyclists to wear helmets. Maybe the police finally got tired of looking at the bikers' faces. In any case, it sparked protests, largely due to the added expense of having to buy said helmets.

The reaction to the new law shows how much Chadians love their motorcycles, or *"motos."* They're the poor man's car, the richer man's bicycle. And they're ubiquitous in the country. It's like Yamaha gave them out for free with the purchase of any large soda.

The *motos* own the streets of N'Djamena. They weave in and out of traffic practicing to be kamikaze pilots. They circle larger vehicles like minnows around a shark, riding in their wake, sidling up next to them, and balancing on them when stopped at an intersection.

They are not happy minnows, though. Most of the drivers are guilty of "DWI"—"Driving While Irritated." They swerve and cut off fellow *motos*. They yell and sneer at others. Even their bikes have filthy mouths as they honk like they're cursing other drivers. I've come to believe Chad is one of the pioneers of road rage—"Mad Max-style"—given the condition of most forms of transportation.

There's little courtesy or civility out there. It's every fish for himself.

Chad, a large, jigsaw-puzzle-piece-shaped country in Central Africa, is not just a bad driver. It's schizophrenic. More precisely, it has a split personality. Most of its psychosis is rooted in its location. It is yet another country that can thank the brilliant European strategists for marking its boundaries with little rhyme or reason.

Like its neighbors in the Sahel, Chad is on the border of Black and Arab Africa. As a result, it doesn't really know who it is or what it's supposed to be. It is politically, economically, culturally, religiously, linguistically, and climatologically ambiguous.

For example, is it African or Arab? Christian or Muslim? Should the people speak French or Arabic? Should they look to sub-Saharan Africa or North Africa for guidance? Is it green and agricultural or a dry, nomadic country?

It's even geographically ambiguous. Is Chad in Central, West or North Africa?

The answer, of course, to all of these questions is "Yes."

Chad is also right on the border between "happy" and "mean" Africa and, these days, leans more toward the latter.

Life's pretty hard in Chad, but I don't think the local demeanor is entirely a matter of deprivation.

There are lots of poor countries that are still able to find happiness. Indeed, such a light countenance describes much of southern and eastern Africa, where people smile easily and sing and dance spontaneously.

Even given names in these regions have a sense of whimsy. It's like their parents live in Victorian England, christening their children "Godfrey," "Humphrey," "Stanley," and "Archibald." They're also big fans of European history. There are first names such as "Churchill" and "Napoleon," even "Hitler" and "Stalin." A figure's ethical reputation apparently doesn't matter much to them, as long as they were famous and powerful. But there are also more charitable names, such as "Chastity," "Honesty," "Goodwill," and "Goodluck."

I've met a man named "Welcome." I imagined his mother thought about the name and said to him, "You're Welcome!"

Then there are the names that don't appear to make any sense. I once saw an interview with a man named "Anymore." Anymore? I can understand a "Many" or "Plenty," but Anymore? It's almost a question. Like the parents didn't know if he was a twin. So when he was born, they asked, "Anymore in there?"

In a place like Chad, those in power set the tone for the rest of the country. And at the moment, Northerners run the government. And they're not happy-go-lucky folks.

In fact, the further north you go in Africa, the less happy the people get. Their version of the world is more severe. They make Russians look like the "Welcome Wagon Lady." Once, the presidential guards in N'Djamena even shot at the US Ambassador's wife who had stopped to take a photo near the palace.

The situation in modern Chad is comparable to China in the sixties when people bought Mao suits to emulate the leader. Thus, most in Chad have adopted the scowl to wear around town these days.

There's much to scowl about though. Chad's a hard place to live.

Chad is the 157th (out of 185) poorest country in the world. About half of the people live below the poverty line.

The land is hot and dry, largely savannah and desert, though some greenery grows in the southern parts. The country recently discovered oil, but there are few other natural resources. The economy is largely pre-modern, most of the farming subsistence-level. There are droughts and locusts. One of the country's most important exports is livestock. Just having a Ministry of Livestock must qualify it as a Third World country.

Chad boasts a massive, life-giving, eponymous lake in the west, which seems to taunt the surrounding desert. It is the equivalent of God throwing the country a bone. The government would probably sell the lake if there were a way.

Like most of its neighbors, Chad has killed, dug up, or chopped down most of its natural resources.

Regardless, little has been done with the income generated from selling its resources to help the country. There are few good roads, schools, hospitals, water or electric systems.

Perhaps the most obvious effect to outsiders is in tourism. Since few large animals exist anymore, safaris are hard to find in Chad, unlike other parts of Africa, which means few tourist groups show up and spend large amounts of money in the country.

Some of the neighbors are even worse off. To the north and west, Niger is the 180th poorest country in the world, making Chad and Niger the Alabama and Mississippi of Africa. Niger usually beats out Chad in the "worse off" department. So Chad comes out looking better, relatively speaking, and can always say, "Thank God for Niger!"

After the Europeans got a whiff of Africa centuries ago, even Chad had to be divvied up, though it probably went in the final round of the draft. Chad is like the last awkward kid who is reluctantly picked in a basketball game—with France finally mumbling, "Oh, alright, we'll take him. But we won't let him play much."

Despite all these downsides, many still want to be in charge of Chad. Go figure. So there has been plenty of terrorism, insurrection, rebellions, and civil war. It's like a bunch of stray dogs fighting over the last bone in a garbage dump.

In 2006, a rebel group, the appropriately-acronymed "FUC," laid siege to the capital. Fighting was so indiscriminate, bulldozers were deployed to clear dead bodies off the street in front of the US embassy.

Large-scale fighting has subsided these days, but security concerns remain. When posted to the country, US officials are not allowed to travel, overland, outside the capital without a really good reason—and an armed convoy.

Conditions like these make me wonder why a country like Chad has things like a Ministry of Tourism and what its head does all day. (Other countries apparently recognize this futility and lump multiple functions into one "Ministry of Youth, Sport, and Tourism.")

For many expats in N'Djamena, life revolves around a few restaurants, a tennis club, and a rudimentary "golf course." And while some of the menus look appetizing, hygiene is—shockingly—not a big priority. I've never been sicker in any country in my life. In Chad, I got to look at all of my partially-digested stomach contents on a regular basis. This is one of those places where you can't really judge whether or not you liked a restaurant until a day or two later.

I should've gotten the hint about the hygiene from the number of flies around. Because it doesn't matter where you go, every time you eat outside in N'Djamena, swarms of the pesky little buggers will try to share your meal. As a result, you usually eat with one hand and shoo them away with the other. If you're in between bites, you put a napkin over your plate and glass. If you don't, dozens of flies will immediately land in your food and drink.

And there are so many more insects around.

Once, while flying out of the country, a few giant cockroaches tried to stowaway in my seat. They were far too big to squish, so I took the complimentary case full of comb, toothbrush, and eye shades, emptied it out, and scooped up the bugs inside. I zipped the case back up and shook it to make sure that the little "visitors" were safely packed away. Whoever opened the packet next surely had a big surprise.

Chad is also the only country I've ever been in without a single mall or department store. There are a few small grocery stores, but if you need to get, say, a pair of tennis shoes or even sunglasses, you're out of luck. I suggested buying the latter at an outdoor market, but a friend warned that some of the glasses sold there are such poor quality that they actually reflect the sunlight back into your eyes.

The primitive conditions at the N'Djamena "golf course" bring new meaning to the phrase "being in the rough." The first time I visited the course, a man was beating his horse in the parking lot. The horse tried to pull away, but fell backwards. Meanwhile, the man continued to beat it while it lay on the ground. Experiences like these lead many to entertain in their homes.

Some expats still find Chad charming, even exotic. To them, it's "old school Africa." It's definitely off the beaten path. Few will ever visit, let alone find it on a map. That's a big motivation for those who want "to boldly go where (almost) no one's gone before." It's like writing your life on a clean sheet of paper, instead of one already blackened with ink. Chad is largely blank—while a place like Thailand is covered in doodles. Just remember, there's a reason no one wants to visit.

To paraphrase a line from the movie *Vacation*: "You think you hate it now, wait till you go there!"

Despite those crazy expats, it's a stretch to call a place like Chad "exotic." Somehow that doesn't seem right. To me, an "exotic" country is located, unfortunately, in the Third World, but it also has palm trees, beaches, and, usually, animals. In an exotic country, you can see elephants wandering in the bush, colorful parrots in the trees. Club Med resorts belong there. If it has a major river, you say "river" before its name, as in the River Nile, or the River Ganges. Which is how I know the Midwest is not especially exotic. No one says the "River Ohio."

So the adjective "exotic" evokes a kind of modern-day Garden of Eden. It's a place you go to on vacation—granted, an exotic vacation—but nevertheless.

I don't think you can refer to countries like Somalia or Iraq with this moniker, either. They're in the same boat with Chad. How can a war-torn nation, ravaged by famine and terrorism, be called "exotic?" No one will ever build a Club Med there.

Don't worry too much about Chad. There are plenty of other adjectives to describe it. You can borrow a few from the book title.

And it could always be worse. Thank God for Niger!

Chapter Three

Farid Flintstone

Afghanistan

You can take the boy out of the cave, but you can't take the cave
out of the boy.
—Unknown

Traveling to some countries means going back in time. Airports
and borders are like doorways to the past.

In Afghanistan, you hop in a really big time machine that puts
the DeLorean to shame, transporting you clear back to the Stone
Age, a world that exists only in books and cartoons.

Afghanistan, in truth, is "The Land That Time Forgot." It's not
just primitive or premodern. In many ways, it's prehistoric. In the
best light, it's a "Modern Stone-Age Family," and a highly dys-
functional one at that.

When I say it's the Stone Age, I mean—literally. Mr. Flint-
stone's job is secure at the Afghan Rock and Gravel Company.
They use the stuff for all sorts of things—to build houses, walls,
roads, and to throw at each other. Although, I never saw cars made
from the stuff. That would be ridiculous. No one can afford a car in
Afghanistan.

Afghanistan is the prehistoric rebuttal to the modern age. Many things you imagine were around in Neolithic times are here today.

In the countryside, most work is done by hand. Water comes from a well, not a tap. Farming is powered by animals, not machines. Food is grown by the family and clothes are made at home, not bought at a store. Need to go somewhere? They will likely walk or take a donkey.

The traditions too are largely the same as in the past. Formal education is considered by many a waste of time. Children need to work and help take care of the family. That's one of the reasons why Afghans have so many of them. The more they have, the more they can do and earn for the family.

But they still marry off a few of the kids when they're, well, kids, some as young as eight. Because they need that dowry something fierce. And they marry them to people that they know, often really well, since they're also first cousins.

It's a male-dominated society, within which women are to be seen, but just barely, and definitely not heard. Under the Taliban, it was a crime for them to laugh out loud in public. They are covered up, head to toe, in baby blue "Darth Vader"-type costumes. They look like giant, pale blueberries. And why not? After all, they are valuable "possessions" which must be protected. The burkas, even the baby blue ones, serve to transform the humans underneath them into less provocative, generic "items," commodities that few would want to touch or take.

They rely on their village. Which is a good thing, since they may well never leave. They trust only their tribe. Outsiders are suspicious. They often fight with them. They are different, so they are bad. They hold grudges and feuds that last for decades. Afghans are the South Asian version of the Hatfields and McCoys.

This is all a shame, since, on the surface, Afghanistan is a magnificent country, one of the most beautiful in the world.

Mountains, mountains, and more mountains. It is the place for those who like the nose bleed section.

And sand. No matter the elevation, desert covers most of the country, especially in the north, south, center, and west. Flying overhead, you can see tiny settlements, some no more than a few houses, which lie at the bottom of dry, brown valleys. Such villages look like green caterpillars searching for the last trace of water. The people within skirt along the edge of survival.

The northeast is greener, often tree-covered and unspoiled. There are few roads and few roadbuilders brave enough to ply their trade. Outsiders, no matter what their intentions, are not welcome. Snow crowns the peaks and rivers flow in the valleys. The scenery looks idyllic. If this were virtually any other country, there would be ski resorts dotting the sides of the mountains.

Afghanistan, perhaps naturally, has a more raw and primitive beauty. It is picturesque in the same way that a volcano is considered lovely.

Its beauty is only skin-deep. The insides are a bit scarier.

Afghanistan is like a Bengal tiger. From a distance, she is extraordinary. But if you try to get close and touch her, even feed her, she will rip out your throat.

Life in Afghanistan, just like the prehistoric days, is dangerous. And when its government is weak, it's also "solitary, poor, nasty, brutish, and short." Right on, Mr. Hobbes.

Life in fictional "Bedrock" was far better, even if the sofas were made out of stone and Fred had to wear the same shirt-dress every day.

In Afghanistan, there are just so many ways you can die. It may be the most dangerous place in history. Let me count the ways:

There are, of course, the extremist groups. You have the ambitious ones seeking to control the whole country, and those who just want to kill others they don't think belong. There are a lot of folks on this list.

And it's not just the big guys you've heard of. There are many different groups in Afghanistan. Thousands and thousands of fighters. And there are lots more waiting on deck, inside and outside the country. A million potential understudies. Most sign up just for the paycheck. Where else can they earn a few hundred dollars a month in an otherwise destitute land?

The place is so bad, almost everyone's armed and everything's booby-trapped in some way.

Even stray animals. In my time there, the extremists filled dead dogs with IEDs, or improvised explosive devices, leaving them on the side of the road to hit a NATO or government vehicle. It was literal roadkill.

Even the ground is armed. There are millions of unexploded anti-personnel mines of every shape and size buried after decades of war. They are in cities and villages, in fields, on roads and paths. During floods, rivers pick up those close to the surface and carry them downstream, making swimming and bathing treacherous. The country has been described as "one big minefield." If out walking around, you never want to pull a "Neil Armstrong" and be the first person to step on any patch of ground. Even in populated areas, you never know what's still lying underneath.

Bombs have branched out into other household items as well. Today, there are even BBIEDs—that's right, bicycle-born explosives. And you thought your bike was bad-ass.

So mortars fly through the air, bombs wait on the surface, and landmines rest underground. Even rivers can explode. Have the extremists covered all the bases? So it seems.

But nope. There's so much more. We haven't even looked at the natural world yet, and in Afghanistan, even Nature is one mean mother.

She brings, for example, deadly malaria, poisonous cobras, scorpions the size of your fist, freezing cold, excruciating heat, and violent monsoon storms.

Scorpions crawled in through holes in the walls of our housing. Cobras slithered inside the shower pipes, came out the drains, and wandered the halls.

The monsoon storms belonged in a Fourth of July fireworks show. During a good one, the wind blows like a hurricane, while the rain falls in giant cluster bombs. Lightning blinks every half second like someone is flipping a switch on and off, over and over, for hours.

(As an aside, Afghanistan's not normally a funny country, but there are still absurdities to laugh at. For example, in the summer, a truck drove the streets of our army base, sprinkling water on the ground to help keep down the dust. One day, an afternoon storm brought a flood of rain. Nevertheless, there he was, right on time, slowly dropping his load on the street—while it was raining. The Afghan driver had a job to do and wasn't going to let a little thing like common sense get in the way.)

But back to mean old Mother Nature.

Mudslides bury whole villages in summer. Avalanches have the same effect in winter.

Earthquakes happen at any time of the year and knock down what few buildings you were able to put up.

Even the beverages are dangerous. When meeting with Afghan government counterparts, we were, hospitably, offered cups of hot tea. The only problem was that they were, ostensibly, the same cups of tea given to everyone before us. Indeed, you could witness the server "clean" the glasses by pouring a small amount of tea in one, swirling it around, dumping the remainder into the next, and repeating this process for the rest of the tray. We called it an "Afghan dishwasher." And the drinks? "Herpes tea." Which is why I usually asked for a Coke.

In Afghanistan, everyone and everything are at their worst. There are no gentle summer showers. No fields of just wildflowers. Every day is a Monday. Every Monday is a bad hair day.

I don't understand why so many have fought so hard for so long for such a country.

Beginning with the earliest folks. Why was Alexander the Great so anxious to get here and why did he fall in love with the place? He chose this over lounging on a Greek island? I would've stayed in Europe.

And, if that weren't enough, not only is Afghanistan, itself, a bad neighborhood, it's also located in a bad neighborhood. Maybe even a worse neighborhood than itself, depending on who you talk to, and how they assign blame for the country's problems.

Afghanistan is surrounded by the toughest bullies on the block. Those who give it constant noogies and never want to see it grow up and do better than they will. Iran, Pakistan, Turkmenistan, Tajikistan, Uzbekistan, Ickistan, Trashcanistan . . . You get the picture.

Some of these countries harass Afghanistan more than others, but most want to push it around at least a little. When you yourself are poor and hopeless, it feels good to have someone, anyone, smaller and poorer to beat up and shake down, even if they only have a little milk money.

Why should this be surprising? Most Third World countries have few real friends. They are reflections of humans in this way. It's tough to keep a friend, or to be a friend, until you have met your own needs. Just like it's hard to be happy for someone until you're happy with yourself. Until then, you're wary, jealous, even hateful, of everyone around you. After all, you live in a precarious world where your neighbors are your competition for the, seemingly, last scraps of bread. There exists a constant threat, a persistent paranoia that they may try to take what little you have. While others, on occasion, may help you survive when it's in their interests, they're just as happy to turn on you.

In some cases, Afghanistan's neighbors take a different approach and try to sell stuff. This probably won't turn out much better. Afghanistan has little to give in return for the Iranian oil,

Pakistani cement, "Dellta" (sic) computers, or "Hond" (sic) motor-cycles from who knows where that you see in the country. (By the way—"Hond"—really? Where did you come up with that brilliant name? What a lazy knock-off. You're not even trying!)

The sale of cell phones has been one, astoundingly, bright spot in the Afghan economy. Over fifty percent of Afghans have them. The use of these phones, however, seems anachronistic in a place where two-thirds of the population are illiterate. It's like Afghanistan entered the twenty-first century before passing the fifteenth. In its extreme, it's a bizarre version of *The Jetsons*. In this episode, George has an apartment in the sky full of robots, but he doesn't know how to read the *TV Guide*.

The reality is that most Afghans have little money to buy anything. There are few jobs and almost no industry. Agriculture is primitive and small-scale.

Of the cash crops that do exist, the biggest one is illegal. At least, in theory.

There are just too many people involved in its production and trade to fully enforce the law. Too much demand from multiple consumers. Too few security personnel who really care. Too much money to be made.

In sum, the country's too poor to turn down such a lucrative business. Even if it's an extremely dangerous drug.

Of course, this wonder drug is opium. And it works wonders.

Afghanistan makes billions of dollars each year from opium production. Millions of Afghans are completely dependent on it for income.

The poppy problem is rampant. In western Afghanistan, they grow in the open. You can see them waving in the wind from the road.

Once, on a drive in northwest Afghanistan, near the Turkmeni-stan border, dozens of young Afghans were walking along the high-way, most carrying backpacks. "That's strange," I thought. "Why are so many out for a hike in the middle of nowhere, especially when it's cold and snowy?"

Turns out, they were carrying opium in their packs, direct from the fields, to be smuggled across the border to Iran and Turkmenistan.

At first, it seemed strange that the smugglers would be so open about it. But I realized that there's not much illegal about this illegal trade. Poppies grow in the open, so why not transport them openly?

Indeed, those assigned "to serve and to protect" are usually just serving themselves and protecting the criminals.

I saw this first-hand as we approached an Afghan police checkpoint not far from the border. Officers were flagging down trucks headed to Turkmenistan to, ostensibly, check their papers. This being Afghanistan, however, the true purpose was more nefarious.

It was a good old-fashioned shakedown. The police demanded that the trucks give them money in exchange for permission to pass on to the border. Everyone knows the routine.

This time, however, a new variable was introduced into the equation—four gringos in an armored truck with government plates.

As we got closer to the checkpoint, a policeman raised his hand to stop a truck approaching from the other direction. At the same time, the officer glanced over his shoulder, saw us, and must've understood that we knew what he was about to do.

The officer responded with a sheepish, sideways grin. He looked back at the truck and promptly waved him through. The driver was a lucky guy this time.

And, at least on that occasion, a police shakedown was put off for another day.

Chapter Four

The Egyptian Brake

Egypt

The single biggest problem in communication is the illusion that
it has taken place.
—Attributed to George Bernhard Shaw

On an event-free, two-mile ride from downtown Cairo to a nearby
suburb, the taxi driver honked his horn over one hundred times.

Fortunately, he didn't have one of those annoying
"EEEEEEHHHHHH . . . . EEEEEEHHHHHH!!"-sounding horns.
He had changed his ringtone to a gentle "ding-ding . . . . ding-
ding."

At first, the sound made me think the driver had run over an old
lady on her bicycle, but then I saw that his wrist was glued to the
middle of the steering wheel.

The mild ringtone seemed out of place on the gritty streets of
Cairo. I imagined that a judge had ordered him to replace his old
horn as a kind of punishment for an excessive-honking violation.
But, let's face it, this is the last thing that would happen in Egypt.

Why would anyone count the number of honks?

The car horn is the most important form of communication in
Cairo. What other device so defines and expresses modern Egyp-

tian culture? And Egyptians love to express themselves. They will
not be ignored. The horn is the way they, well, toot their own horn.

Forget Facebook. If Mubarak wanted to suppress communication, he should've banned the car horn.

The horn is the original social media, the loudest, most immediate device for yelling, "Look at me!" Egyptians have made it into
an art form and a national pastime. Perhaps even the national an-
them.

It's the ideal communication device for the local environment.
After all, Cairo is not what you'd call a walking city. The automo-
bile is the only reasonable way to get around. Everyone else is in
the same boat—or car—in this case. And this is the way you stay in
touch with others around you.

There is every reason to honk, and almost no reason not to. It is
used as both an overt and a subtle form of communication.

If the band REM were Egyptian, they'd have a famous song
called "Everybody Honks."

Let's look at a few examples. Egyptians honk:

When they pick you up or drop you off.

To say "Thanks" or "Go to Hell," or "Thanks for going to Hell."
When another car's too close. When it's too far away.

When they turn, when they don't turn, when they thought about
turning but decided not to, when they're going straight and have no
intention whatsoever of turning in the next two hours.

When they see a pretty girl, or a not so pretty girl, or, really, any
girl, or even when they remember a girl they saw yesterday.

When they're going in reverse against traffic on a crowded high-
way—this happens more often that you'd think—and the honk is
meant to also say, "Thanks for giving me room to drive like a
lunatic today and not smashing into me!"

To remind the driver in front that the light is about to turn green
and he should start going . . . NOW! Indeed, if a driver actually

waited until it was green to go, the honks would rain down like a summer hail storm.

Finally, Egyptians honk, sometimes, just because they haven't honked in a while and they miss hearing the sound of their car's "voice."

And don't think that if you've heard one horn, you've heard them all. Oh no, there are a million honks in this fair city. The worst are the high-pitched ones. These crawl up your spine, make your head want to explode, and reduce your life expectancy.

Most Americans aren't used to this level of inter-automotive communication. Blowing your horn back home is often seen as a hostile act that shatters world peace. You might as well have fired an Uzi into the air. Even in major cities, American honking has a specific purpose, a defined time frame, a beginning and an end.

But not in Cairo. There are just so many others to talk to.

Traffic is an epic, apocalyptic ballet. Jams can last all day and turn driving into chess-like decisions. Cars move and sway, sashay back and forth, trying to figure out which side is moving faster, or will in the next two minutes, and which of their fellow autos might be kind, or oblivious, enough to let them in.

The Cairo cars fill in empty spaces like a stream flowing downhill. Dotted lines, as the cliché goes, are mere suggestions, and, in reality, you can cruise wherever you want. On the road. Off the road. In between lanes. With traffic. Against it. You can go just about anywhere, except in your own lane. Any move or measure is authorized if it will save you a few seconds.

And there's no "your space" or "my space" on the road. What's yours is mine and what's mine is ours. But it's all really just ours, or at least whoever gets there first. Two-lane roads turn into three, with the sidewalk useful as a passing lane. Cairo brings reality to the joke, "If you don't like the way I drive, stay off the sidewalks!"

In the end, all these techniques allow more cars to squeeze in. Because Egyptian roads are like an Irish family—"There's always room for one more."

Don't be fooled by this apparent folly. Despite the insanity, Egyptians take their cars and their driving seriously. The ballet can turn into a boxing match in an instant if you happen to run into another dancer.

On birthdays, I imagine Egyptian parents giving their kid a toy car with a starter horn. Like putting a baseball mitt in the crib, they hope it will give them a head start on other drivers.

But let's not be exclusive. Adults could use them in their homes, too. Want something from your wife? Blow a portable horn to get her attention. Someone's in your easy chair? "Hooonnnnk!" Or, conversely, want to listen to something soothing at the end of the day? Don't bother with "Sounds of the Whale." Put on the country's latest hit while gently dozing off . . . "Songs of the Car Horn!"

On a deeper level, the horn is an existential item Egyptians could not live without. It is a personal declaration that says, "I honk, therefore I am!"

Perhaps my saddest taxi ride came when I saw a car horn finally die. It was a like strange version of a Don Mclean song.

We were half-way to our destination when it gave its last beep. I looked at the driver, wondering what he would do next. He was panicked and confused. How could he drive so naked and defense-less? Something must be done.

While still moving, he pulled out a screwdriver from the glove box and popped off the horn's cover. He looked inside but had no idea what to do next. Clearly radical, reconstructive surgery was required. He would need a "horn-ectomy."

So he did what any red-blooded Egyptian man would do next. He put the cover back on and started hitting the horn with the screwdriver, succeeding only in scratching up the steering wheel. Meanwhile, the desperation grew on his face.

For the rest of the trip, he reflexively pressed the horn when someone cut him off, slamming his hand the worse it got, though nothing came out. Not a peep.

Others could talk to him, but he could not respond. He yelled out the window, sounding like the Tasmanian Devil, but it had no effect. The other cars didn't speak his language. He was a mute piece of metal going down the street. You could see it in his face. He slowly became irrelevant. A part of him had died, along with his horn.

"My kingdom for a horn!" I could almost hear him cry.

Chapter Five

A Quick Geography Lesson

Bulgaria

> When Brian told me he grew up in New Mexico, I told him I
> thought it is cool that people from other countries play football.
> —Terry Bradshaw

Bulgaria is like the "Bizarro-Europe." They don't say "Hello" when they leave. But they do nod when they mean "No" and shake their head for "Yes."

In fact, outside of the continent, many people don't know where Bulgaria is, let alone that it's even in Europe.

Don't believe me? Go ahead, ask the person next to you if she knows where it's located. For a bonus point, ask her to name two countries that border it.

My Bulgarian neighbor in Sofia once whispered to me in the hallway that he was "black." I looked at his white skin and politely nodded my head, which only added to the confusion.

"You are the whites," he clarified, pointing at my chest. "We are the blacks. We are the Africans. Everyone thinks Bulgaria is located somewhere down there."

I was skeptical of his claim. After all, he's the same guy who told me there were three groups that secretly controlled everything in the world—the Jews, the Freemasons, and some other group, which he couldn't remember that day.

"That's preposterous," I thought. "Others must know where Bulgaria is. At the very least, that it's in Europe."

Later, a telephone operator in the US proved his point.

An American friend was having difficulty calling home over the holidays. He finally reached the operator and, in frustration, said, "I need help, ma'am. I'm calling from Bulgaria and can't get through. Do you even know where that is?" "Of course I know where Bulgaria is, sir," she replied defiantly. "It's in Africa!"

Case closed.

A small, Lego-shaped country about the size of Pennsylvania, Bulgaria is in Europe—but just barely. It squeezed into the southeast corner of the continent when no one else was looking. The country's like a runner who inches past the remainder of the field—Turkey, Georgia, Armenia—to finish third and win a medal. They made it in just under the wire. They're on "the good side of the tracks."

Bulgaria is a Byzantine-type place, probably best known for its roses, yoghurt, and for sending an assassin to kill the Pope.

It is the last outpost before taking a giant leap into Turkey, the Middle East and Asia. After that, it all goes downhill real fast—I mean, gets more exotic—as you head into Iran, Afghanistan, Pakistan . . . need I go on?

Bulgaria guards the southeast corner of Europe but, culturally at least, doesn't feel much like it's in it, or of it. The country has, historically, been pulled more east than west. Perhaps this is logical, since its ancient ancestors came from southern Russia.

It's the poster child for the slogan, "Geography is destiny." Its location has been both a blessing and a curse. Though mostly a curse, which we will look at later.

This can be seen in its history, which has also been a curse. Or, perhaps, just bad luck. To be fair, some of the troubles were self-inflicted.

But there were still some good times.

Virtually every country has a "Golden Age," a time when they were a great power, even an empire. It doesn't matter how small the place.

These times are a source of national pride, even when they occurred hundreds or thousands of years ago. In most cases, this pride is out of proportion to what they've done lately. Who can name one Iranian accomplishment in the last two thousand years? The hookah doesn't count.

But maybe that explains why they hold on so tight to the past. Sometimes you have to go with what you've got.

It's like a Cubs fan still commemorating the 1908 World Series. But even they're not that sentimental.

Bulgaria is no exception to the rule. Like Persia and Greece, its glory days are long gone, but that doesn't stop it from remembering them like they were yesterday.

Bulgaria was a big fish in the Middle Ages, when its empire stretched north into Romania, west to the Adriatic, and south to the Aegean. But soon, the neighbors wanted empires too, and Bulgaria lost much of its territory.

History is different in the Balkans. In a sense, there's no such distinct discipline. History is, instead, one long, uninterrupted chain of days and years that lead up to the present.

As a result, Balkan people feel their ancestors closely. It doesn't matter if they lived one or one thousand years ago. They consider them the same people, the same tribe, one big extended family. They just happened to exist at a different time.

Where else but in the Balkans would you see fresh graffiti about a battle that was lost over six hundred years ago? Now that's a grudge!

Americans are amateurs in this department. We're taught to not live in the past. To live even in the present is often discouraged. We must be on the move, looking ahead, constantly reinventing ourselves. We're not supposed to be in a state of "being," but, rather, "becoming."

One result is we're quick to forgive, forget, and rebuild the last country we defeated.

We're like parents who spank a child for being bad but then buy him an ice cream—and a new power plant!—because we want him to learn his lesson and move out someday.

Can you imagine if we still resented the British?

Ironically, the ones we fought the hardest are our closest friends today.

Bulgaria has no such mentality, and has the street names to prove its devotion to the past. There are boulevards, roads, and throughways that honor czars from the seventh century—over thirteen hundred years ago. Indeed, people fight and die over territorial designations in the Balkans, so names are serious business. (Just ask The Former Yugoslav Republic of Macedonia. "Thanks for blocking the shorter version, Greece. That just rolls off the tongue.") Most streets are christened after famous leaders and the dates on which they did great things. You will not see a "Sycamore Street" or an "Apple Dumpling Lane."

There are, however, some Bulgarian place names which must've been chosen by someone with a drinking problem. For example, there is a suburb of Sofia called "The Refrigerator" and another called "Bedbugs." Imagine telling a friend where you live. There is a village in the south simply called "Poor." And housing complexes named "Hope" and "Youth." As in, "I hope I never have to live here." And "Get out while you're still young."

Sofia's motto is "Ever growing, never old." From this punchline, you learn that, when a Balkan country comes up with a slogan, you can be sure that the reality's the complete opposite. After all, if you need to say it, it's probably not true.

Sofia's reality is that it's ancient and elderly. Everything in it, of it, about it, and around it is old. It's full of old people, old cars, and old clothes. It's full of old, crumbling roads and buildings. Behind its back, the capital city is called a "giant village," since it was rapidly populated after World War II by peasants from the countryside. These men and women brought with them "hobbies," such as hocking loogies, shooting snot rockets, burping, urinating in public, and bumping into strangers. Old men pee on the side of the cathedral in the middle of the day. Grandmas spit in the street like they're on their way to a gunfight. And, when they run into you, they don't say, "Excuse me," but rather, "*Opa*," the Bulgarian version of "Whoops!"

In the Late Middle Ages, Bulgaria was ruled by the Ottoman Empire for five hundred years and did not gain independence until 1878. In the meantime, it missed out on virtually every historic European movement, including the Renaissance, the Reformation, the Enlightenment, and the Industrial Revolution.

After independence, Bulgaria sided with the wrong allies, losing four out of five wars, including the Cold War. After the Second World War, the country became part of the Eastern Bloc and was saddled with communism for almost fifty years. This was not necessarily a bad thing, since it helped Bulgaria's largely rural economy become modern and urban relatively quickly.

Perhaps, as a result of this mixed historical record, Bulgarians are bipolar about their status today. They are true manic-depressives.

One moment, they consider themselves the greatest thing since sliced *hlyab*. This manic side marches down the street when the soccer team is about to play another country. "Bulgarians . . . Heroes!" they shout.

Many also believe they are the second-smartest people in the world, after the Israelis. They're the only ones who can outwit them, they tell you.

To demonstrate this point, an American friend who taught high school in a small Bulgarian town told a story about one of his students. The student boldly declared, without any irony or humor, that a Bulgarian had actually discovered America. The teacher asked if he meant that Christopher Columbus wasn't really Italian after all. "Oh no, he was," the student replied. "But the guy who stands up in the . . . what do you call top part of the ship?" "The crow's nest," the teacher responded. "Yeah, the guy up there—he was Bulgarian!"

And yet, at other moments, they are downright depressed about the country. They are self-haters and doubters who, they believe, can't do anything right. When I asked my own university-level classes to name some of the things they were proud of, the question was followed by looks of embarrassment.

Psychologically, Bulgaria went through its own version of a "Great Depression" after the fall of communism. They should've pumped Prozac into the Sofia water system.

In the 1990s, especially, most students had no future. They applied for visas, work permits, and scholarships to foreign universities in desperate attempts to flee the country. They took the SATs, GREs, and TOEFL and did shockingly well, often better than native English speakers.

What was their dirty little secret? Sad to say, many of them cheated. Americans who also took these exams while living in Bulgaria reported that local proctors often left the room, allowing test-takers to pull out their dictionaries and notes and talk over the answers with friends. In any case, many ended up at the best American universities.

Who can blame them for doing whatever it took to get out? Most Americans could never imagine living in a place like Bulgaria. A place with rampant corruption, extortion, and dysfunction. Where even the most basic institutions can't be trusted. Where the police run in the opposite direction when they see a crime. Where elderly people cannot afford to pay the bribes required for treatment at the hospital. Where so-called "banks" go out of business overnight when their owners run off with the money. Where many at the highest levels of power are in cahoots with criminal groups, refusing to enforce the laws or protect the people. Where university students pay bribes to professors for good grades. Where most go home to endless rows of dark, soul-less apartment blocks in the suburbs.

An American friend saw this dysfunction up close in an unusual run-in with one of "Sofia's Finest." He was walking by parliament, of all places, when a police officer grabbed him by the neck, likely for the "crime" of speaking a foreign language to a friend. However, he was quickly released from the long arm of the law when it came out that he was an American. The cop then propositioned him, asking, "Have you tried our beautiful Bulgarian girls yet?" and, "Would you like to get a prostitute?"

In recent years, geography has been a little kinder, as Bulgaria joined NATO and then the EU.

Most Bulgarians don't feel like a part of either. A significant percentage still prefer Moscow over Brussels, despite all the benefits they receive from the latter.

Ordinary folks tend to agree that joining the so-called "Euro-Atlantic Institutions" hasn't helped that much. Money has poured into the country in recent years in the form of investment, aid, loans, and grants. But much of it has been wasted or lost to corruption and inefficiency. Little seems to have trickled down.

Many say the recent changes have been largely cosmetic, like painting over the cracks and holes in a wall. The country is still basically the same—the same ugly blocks, bad roads, overgrown parks, poor service, primitive villages, bad healthcare, and omnipresent stray dogs. Before, there was no money and nothing to buy. Now, there are lots of things to buy, but most cannot afford them.

So where does Bulgaria fit in the grand scheme of things? Under communism, it was labeled a "Second World" country. Where is it today?

In some ways, it has both First and Third World characteristics. For example, in the major cities, there seem to be no shortage of consumer goods and expensive cars. While in the countryside, many farmers still use horse-drawn plows.

To answer this question more easily, I devised the following overly-simplistic test, which I've usually found to be accurate— Can you drink the tap water?

If "Yes," you're likely in a First World country. If "No," you're probably hanging out in the Third World. It's often that simple.

Except, of course, when it's not, like in Bulgaria. Nothing there is ever so transparent. So the answer to the question here is "Maybe."

Technically, most of the tap water is free from harmful bacteria and you can drink it, at least, in the short run. But, in reality, you wouldn't want to for long. Most locals don't even drink it and will tell you to avoid it, since some water contains heavy metals.

So maybe the answer lies somewhere in the middle and Bulgaria should still be considered "Second World," if that's possible.

Indeed, looking at themselves today, many Bulgarians feel they are no better off than their parents when the communists were in power. That being said, rising incomes, visa-free travel, and availability of consumer goods tell a different story. But, after all, it only matters how you feel. And much of this new-found discouragement is due to their perspective.

Bulgaria used to look East (if it looked at all) and compare itself to fellow communist countries. Most were at about the same level. The comparison was largely meaningless, anyway, since there wasn't much they could do to progress.

Now, however, as members of the EU, Bulgarians look West, where the grass is unbelievably greener. In contrast, they feel weak and poor, even though they're better off than they used to be. After all, you can be a millionaire and still feel poor if your neighbors are all billionaires.

As with my own neighbor, however, perhaps the source of the angst is more cultural. Most Bulgarians I've met don't feel European. In this way, they're more like the Russians—an amalgamation of the East and the West, half Asian and half European, but all of neither, and, therefore, confused about their true identity. Like Chad, it is schizophrenia on a national level. But that's a topic for another "session."

In the end, maybe it's normal that foreigners don't know where the country is located. Most Bulgarians don't seem to know either.

Chapter Six

Friendly Fire

Afghanistan

The greatness of a nation can be judged by the way its animals are treated.
—Attributed to Mahatma Gandhi

The US Army has used dogs in wartime since the early nineteenth century. In recent years, hundreds have served in Iraq and Afghanistan, tracking militants and detecting bombs, often risking their lives.

Not all of them were drafted.

Duke was a volunteer in eastern Afghanistan. He had wandered onto the army base in Konar Province like other local hounds, ducking under the metal gate, looking for food. A Yellow Lab, he stood out from the other dogs.

One day, Duke started following the American soldiers when they went on patrol. Though untrained, he barked when he detected Taliban fighters in the tall grass, often before the soldiers saw them. He became a regular part of the team, taking point on patrols. A sergeant praised him for saving their lives many times. Duke was eventually given a name and tied to a post on base, which meant that someone was looking after him, at least from time to time.

I brought Duke treats from the mess hall after lunch. Showing off his Western ways, he loved ham sandwiches—hold the bread. He would gulp them down in one bite and go for my fingers as dessert. Nevertheless, Duke remained a lot like Afghanistan—stoic, beautiful, hard to know. Even when happy, he only wagged his tail a few inches back and forth.

Unfortunately, Duke also barked at the Afghans who worked on base and, when he got loose, nipped at their heels. Eventually, the locals complained to the higher-ups. One time, they took matters into their own hands and beat Duke with a shovel. A dog-friendly medic sewed up his bleeding head.

Our friendship lasted several weeks until, one day, I didn't see Duke after lunch. I walked to his usual hangout and asked a soldier where the dog was. "Duke? Oh, they shot him this morning," he said casually. "Army's getting rid of all the strays."

NOTE

This essay was originally published in Arcadia Magazine 9.3 (2015): 116.

Chapter Seven

Chester

Egypt

Our God is a God of second chances—Yes, God does these
things again and again for people.
—Job 33:29

After leaving Afghanistan, I met one of Duke's long-lost cousins in
Egypt.

Chester, like Duke, had brown eyes and fuzzy yellow hair and
was employed in security—this time as a bomb sniffer at a hotel in
Cairo.

I passed the hotel each day while walking to work. If Chester
was on duty, I'd stop and play with him, give him biscuits and
words of encouragement. These were especially important, since he
had a hard life.

Chester and five other dogs—Hector, Simba, Caesar, Buddy,
and Max—were assigned to a parking lot where they screened cars
arriving at the hotel. They were either chained up, or on a leash,
twenty-four hours a day, whether working outside in the hot sun or
sleeping in the basement below the lot. When I played with Chester, he caught tennis balls while chained to a fence.

And I peeked once inside the basement. Bad idea. It was a nasty place. Dogs were tied up, eating and sleeping close to their own waste, surrounded by flies. It was a real doggy-dungeon.

Chester wagged his tail the first time he saw me coming down the sidewalk, as if we already knew each other. I was taken aback at his resemblance to Duke and the subtle ways he showed affection.

As I went to leave, he stepped on my foot, looked at me, and tried to speak. He didn't growl or bark. He gave out a long, low grumble, like Chewbacca would have done.

(I later understood that Chester was a true Egyptian in expression. He grumbled when he was hungry. He grumbled when he was fed. Whether happy or sad, he had to tell you about it. And he was never fully satisfied.)

But, at that moment, I knew he was special, as if there were already a bond between us. If there is love at first sight with animals, this was it. Or maybe it was just a chance to renew a friendship with an old companion.

Fortuitously, Chester, unlike Duke, had been drafted into service and was no good at his job. He was not on the "A-Team." In fact, he was—cover your ears, big guy—a downright awful bomb dog, who preferred looking at the birds in the sky to sniffing under cars for possible explosives. His handler hit him on the head each time he didn't focus. Yet again, like most Egyptians, violence had no effect on him.

Our friendship lasted several months until, one day, his handler said to me, "Chester love you. You loves Chester?" I said, "Of course, he's a great dog." "You want Chester?" he asked quickly.

I was incredulous, thinking for a moment, that he was just going to hand him over then and there. Or maybe that it was all just a cruel joke.

It wasn't a joke, he was willing to let the dog go. But, no, he wasn't free. I'd have to pay for him. This was still Egypt, after all. No one gives anything away.

Indeed, to the hotel, Chester was simply a piece of property that had become obsolete and was being sold. To me, however, it seemed like he was being ransomed, since I had no idea what would happen if I didn't take him.

Either way, I felt like I was about to take the concept of rescuing a dog to a whole new level. Not only would I get him out of a bad life, I would, in essence, be buying his freedom. After all, Chester was not simply an unwanted stray that would be adopted for a nominal fee. He was a pure breed and a "trained" bomb sniffer, although he must've slept through most of his classes. And, perhaps as a result, the payoff turned out to be—not a small amount of money. The handler knew his target well.

I would have to talk it over with the wife.

Both of us hemmed and hawed, coming up with every possible excuse not to adopt Chester. "Cairo is no place to raise a dog." "The city is a dirty, polluted mess." "There is little green space and almost no room to run." "The landlady (like most Egyptians) is not dog-friendly."

We added up all the reasons and went with the easy decision. No, we could not adopt Chester. It would just be too hard.

I went back to the hotel and gave the handler the bad news. I left with my tail between my legs, knowing that, once again, I had failed to save a dog in need.

A few days later, I stopped to pet Chester after work. As I approached the hotel, the handler was "playing" with him by stepping on his feet. All he could do was try to pull them away.

The dog looked at me as I walked home. I was ashamed of myself.

And that was enough for me. I finally snapped. I got home and said to my wife, "We have to go get Chester."

After a few days of negotiating with the hotel, we made arrangements to pick him up after work.

It felt like a late-night prison-break.

We arrived at the parking lot as instructed. My wife was the bagman. We paid the money and waited for the dog. The handler went down into the basement. I could hear him unchain Chester. The other dogs barked as one of their lucky colleagues was taken out. I saw Chester come slowly up the stairs, looking groggy and confused—it wasn't time for his shift. But his tail started wagging when he saw us. He had no idea that his whole life was about to change.

I yanked off his smelly, old collar and snapped on a brand new one. I quickly put him in our truck and drove away before anyone could change their mind—or ask for more money.

We took Chester to the vet, where he got a full check-up, shots, a hot bath, and a haircut.

On the way home, he stuck his head out the window and let the warm air hit his face, probably seeing more of the city than he ever had before.

And so, Chester, instead of being eliminated like Duke, was allowed to retire peacefully. We brought him into our family, our home, and our world. He had won the "Green Card Lottery." He was no longer a prisoner. Just like that, he was free.

We went back to our apartment and he hit his head on the glass door to the building, thinking it was open. In the lobby, there was a wall of mirrors at his level. For probably the first time, he saw his reflection and was aware of himself.

Or, maybe, he saw his cousin, Duke, who, by losing his life, had helped make him free.

Either way, Chester looked in the mirror, did a double-take, and wagged his tail. And grumbled.

Chapter Eight

Just Kidding

Pakistan

Fear makes the wolf appear bigger than he is.
—German proverb

One day, as part of some official protest, the Pakistani government hung a huge banner in front of parliament in the capital, Islamabad, which declared, "Hands Off Kashmir!"

The message was directed at India, Pakistan's historic rival, and its policy in the disputed region. The banner looked serious. The whole country was behind its government. The people were ready for war!

As you got closer, however, you could see another message in the lower left-hand corner, which seemed to minimize the banner's consequence: an advertisement from "The Hair Club for Men."

Apparently, no banner pays for itself.

Or maybe the government was just targeting a different demographic—the balding South Asians.

And that's one of the takeaways from the country. When it comes to Pakistan, you have to look at the fine print.

On the surface, Pakistan seems ultra-mean and deadly. Its reputation ranks it up—or rather down—there with countries such as

Iran and Iraq. Everything's extreme in Pakistan—the religion, the poverty, the disease, the terrorism, the nuclear weapons. Even its extremism is extreme.

Pakistanis are different, after all. They, literally, live on the other side of the world from us. The foreboding "other side of the is-land," as Gilligan used to put it. They are our complete opposites—the "Bizarro Americans." They must be scary people.

And the country's reputation precedes it. You need no warning before you go. You've already made up your mind. You've seen all the scary movies. All the images of religious fanatics waving AK-47s and burning American flags.

Pakistan's the "World's Official Bogeyman." It's out to get you!

When I told a friend I was about to go there, he made a deep guttural sound. "What was that?" I asked. "The belly of the beast," he said. "That's where you're going."

At the time—after 9/11—that was an appropriate jest.

But this reputation is also a guise that's exploited by Pakistanis themselves when useful, and interpreted, over-simplistically, by outsiders as hostile.

Since 9/11, it's like Pakistan's Board of Tourism has been put in reverse. Their PR machine is used to dissuade you from loving or visiting the place.

As such, the country's a tiger that growls and shows its teeth to scare off potential enemies, or potential anyones, for that matter. After going there, however, I realized it's more like a paper tiger. And, unlike Afghanistan, the Pakistani tiger is often funny and absurd, rather than fierce, a regular South Asian version of the comic strip "Hobbes." Ultimately, it's an imaginary being—most of what you "see" is only in your head.

Here's a fun example. Feel like hitting a few golf balls? Head down to the driving range at the Islamabad golf course. It's the one where kids collect the balls, by hand, without any cage, car, or protective gear. It's you against them. Your golf skills against their ability to play the most dangerous game of dodge ball. Because, you imagined right, ball collectors, perhaps inevitably, become targets themselves for some of the more sadistic golfers.

So maybe the country is extreme, after all. Extremely silly.

"But Pakistanis are so different from us," you counter. No, not really.

They may look a little different and, in public, put up an aggressive front, but many are just like you and me.

For example, Pakistani Muslims are not supposed to drink alcohol, but many still enjoy a sip every now and then. As long as it's behind closed doors. As a result, there's a thriving local moonshine business. Your empty Johnnie Walker bottles are worth something to bootleggers, who refill them for those who can't afford the real stuff.

In fact, the only Pakistanis legally allowed to consume alcohol are the Christian minority. They must show their identity cards when buying booze to ensure that Muslims are not "corrupting" themselves. And they have kept Murree, the one and only legal Pakistani brewery and distillery, in business since 1860.

The rules are a little different if you're a visitor to the country. You can order a beer via room service at your hotel after signing a two-page consent form that states you need the drink for "medicinal purposes."

Or, at select restaurants in Islamabad, the waiter will bring you clandestine pitchers of beer if you order the "special tea." Al Capone would've been proud.

Indeed, while relatively conservative, Pakistanis listen to music, watch movies, like to dance, and have picnics in the park. Or anywhere there's a little grass, even if it's the median of a highway. They are also family-oriented and believe strongly in education.

"Alright then, Pakistanis hate us, at least." Again—no, not really.

Okay, in all fairness, some may indeed hate our guts. But it's not for the reasons you think.

They don't hate us for what we are—religious infidels, boozers, bacon eaters, whatever. Why would they care what we eat or drink? Having such concerns is a luxury that few Pakistanis can afford.

They hate us, simply, 'cause they ain't us. They want what we have—a big house, cool stuff, money for the family, the means to travel anywhere. They're pissed they can't have these things. So they sometimes take their anger out on us, especially when their leaders tell them it's our fault they have nothing.

Want proof? Every morning in Islamabad, the lines to get a visa to visit, work, or immigrate to America snake around the block, full of Pakistanis who want to move next door to you. To adopt your lifestyle. To become like you.

Ironically, the lines have only gotten longer since 2001.

And it's not just in Pakistan. Those lines for American visas are around the block in just about every country in the world—often longest in the places that supposedly hate us the most.

That's one of the larger lessons from the Third World. Few of the people actually hate the US or our foreign policy. How could they? They don't even know much about the US or our foreign policy, other than we're rich and have a lot of stuff. They hate, or more precisely covet, this stuff. They're angry they can't have it. Hell, they're angry at just about anyone who has more than they do.

"Well then, what about all those anti-American protests in Pakistan?"

Turns out, most of those so-called "protesters" are really just part of your everyday "rent-a-mob"—or a "rag-a-muffin"—as the case may be. They've been paid—in money, lunches, or even free bus rides to the big city—to burn some flags and wave some signs that most didn't write and, probably, can't even read.

You can't believe much of what you see in Pakistan. One time, I had a casual conversation with a local journalist at a reception in

Islamabad, before the eventual war in Iraq. The journalist said that many other countries, including Iran, were against a US invasion. I responded, perhaps a little off-the-cuff, that they seemed to have plenty of their own problems to worry about. The next day, the front page of *The Frontier Post* from Peshawar, "quoting" yours truly, read "US to Attack Iran After Iraq."

To me, Pakistan looked more like an amusing place, more like a retirement home for circus performers. And the people continue to amaze and entertain all those who visit.

To begin with, their dress is often a show in itself. Locals are draped in strange, colorful clothing, probably the same ancient garb they wore when Alexander the Great used to visit. The men's *shalwar kameezes* were affectionately called "man-jammies" by us gringos. They wear curious things on their heads. They paint designs on their hands for special occasions. They have piercings in unusual places. They even put mascara on babies, which makes them look like they're in the cast of a Billy Idol video.

There are a surprisingly large number of midgets and dwarves, giving the country the look of a medieval fair. An American friend would give them rides when they hitchhiked.

But perhaps my favorite part of Pakistan was the barber shops. I actually looked forward to getting a haircut. There, the barbers take a more "hands-on" approach. It's not just a trim but also a chance to take their frustrations out on your head. (Indeed, if you did think Pakistanis hated Americans, perhaps this would, on the surface, be confirmation.) I was startled the first time it happened. The barber put down his clippers and stood behind me. Then, without warning, he started smacking the back of my head. It felt like a little kid was trying to beat me up. But this was followed by a spirited neck rub. The extra blood flow did wonders for my scalp (despite what others might think).

On the downside, some mental and physical disabilities and diseases are unusually high in Pakistan. While it's certainly a controversial subject, doctors have speculated that widespread inbreeding, in which parents are also first cousins, is a possible source of these problems. At one time, the practice was common even in the West—take a look at how diseases like hemophilia plagued the European royal families—but it hangs on in parts of the Third World, especially in the lands between Marrakesh and Bangladesh. Some think that inbreeding even causes a large number of Pakistanis to suffer mild retardation. Now, I'm no doctor, but you notice some of these deformities in the population, such as individuals with six or seven fingers, or even two thumbs, on one hand.

And you enter this world immediately upon landing in Pakistan. You arrive at the airport, leave the terminal, and, just like other countries, are met by hundreds of smiling locals, who appear to be waiting for friends and family. "Why are so many people smiling at me?" you ask yourself. It's like the government hired an army of male Walmart Greeters in *shalwar kameezes* to welcome visitors to the country. Then it hits you. There are entirely too many of them relative to the number of passengers and flights per day.

You learn the strange little secret that most of them are not, in fact, meeting anyone at the airport. At least, anyone they know. They've come simply because it's cheap entertainment. "Cheap?" Hell, it's free! To them, it's like going to the zoo. It's fun to catch a glimpse of the exotic foreigners who have flown in from all around the world—especially the blond ones who aren't covered from head to toe! Maybe it's also a vicarious thrill. While unable to travel themselves, they can, at least briefly, share in the fun of others who do.

In the end, Pakistan does, of course, have unimaginable problems. There are, after all, two hundred million people, most of them poor and uneducated, in a landmass only slightly larger than Texas. The vast majority of them, however, do not hate America and have nothing against you.

And, in case you were wondering, some are aware of their place in world opinion, especially those lucky enough to escape outside. I've met Pakistanis overseas who, when asked where they're from, mumble their country's name under their breath, as if saying the word out loud will cause others to run away in horror.

So, before I went to Pakistan, I believed all the warnings—I was sure it was an extremely serious place. Later, after taking a closer look, I had a hard time taking it seriously. In other words, I went in gritting my teeth and came out grinning.

Maybe that's how every country should be taken. You'll be a happier person. Most won't understand why you're smiling though.

Chapter Nine

Land of the Free

Bulgaria

> The worst enemy of life, freedom, and the common decencies is total anarchy; their second worst enemy is total efficiency.
> —Attributed to Aldous Huxley

Each time I get off the plane in Bulgaria, I feel like a fish that had been caught and then released back into the water. Suddenly, I am free, back in my natural environment, where I belong. In Bulgaria, I can breathe again.

The US is still called "The Land of the Free." But someone, apparently, hasn't checked on its status in years. I think, if you were to use more recent data, you'd see that we officially lost that title a long time ago.

These days, instead of freedom, we choose to honor the virtues of political correctness, stopping climate change, and banning large sodas. We treat everyone like children who must be constantly told how to live their lives.

In doing so, we have now been passed by nearly every Second and Third World country in what we used to do best.

That's right, even those that were once behind the Iron Curtain. The ones notorious for the way they controlled every aspect of their citizens' lives. The ones we used to scorn for being "oppressive" and "totalitarian." Those guys. They have beaten us at our own game. In today's world, everything has come full circle.

Indeed, apart from a handful of "commie holdouts"—Cuba, China, North Korea—virtually every other formerly-communist nation has less restrictions on personal freedom than the US and other advanced economies.

A country like Bulgaria is the new "Land of the Free." And that makes its president, ironically, the true "Leader of the Free World."

Oh well. At least we're still "The Home of the Brave."

The passing of this torch was perfectly natural. After all, you can't argue with evolution. Whether we like it or not, we are on a predetermined course.

What happens when a country reaches a certain tipping point in prosperity? It tries to perfect society, in order to make "progress" reach every corner of the world.

Most countries don't have the luxury of Western concerns. They're too busy trying to put food on the table or worrying that the mob will burn down their business. So they don't think much about the guy who threw trash on the ground or made insensitive comments about his neighbor. These are "First World problems," as the cliché goes.

These Western goals are understandable, even honorable, but they don't take away from the fundamental desire to be free.

In its purest form, there is nothing more powerful than exercising your will. Doing what you want, when you want, is intoxicating. Just ask Nietzsche.

Ironically, most Americans will never be that free. It is this innate desire, however, which often draws Westerners to other parts of the world. They long to have these rights returned to them, even if they don't fully recognize this desire or define their motivation in this way.

Maybe that's one reason why Bulgaria is called "The Wild, Wild East." After all, it's the way the US used to be when we were the "Wild, Wild West"—open and free, full of adventure and opportunity.

Ah, freedom, that gloriously-loaded word that conjures up images of independence, personal choice, and deciding for oneself how to live.

Americans declare that we're free all the time, but until we compare ourselves to places like Bulgaria, we have no idea how far-off that statement is. Maybe we continue to say it because we know it's barely true anymore.

Ironically, Bulgarians don't consider themselves very free and don't usually praise the country in this regard. (But they certainly resist when someone tries to take away some of their "liberties.") They see the concept of freedom in more economic terms. As a result, Bulgarians consider themselves lacking in freedom because the jobs don't exist that will make them prosperous. But I'm not talking about economic freedom. I'm talking personal freedom—to say, do, or be, whomever you choose.

They have the freedom. We have the prosperity. If only we could marry the two. Then again, perhaps they're mutually exclusive.

Relative to the West, Bulgaria is a regular Statue of Liberty. They've got freedom coming out their ears. For example:

Want to go out for a drink but don't have the money for a real date? Grab a two-liter jug of beer and a bag of chips. Sit on a park bench with your friend and watch the people go by. You guessed it. There are no open container laws. And, perhaps more important, no hang ups or guilt trips about alcohol, in general. (Or about nudity, sleeping late, or being late, but those are topics for another time.) That means you can drink just about any place outside of your car. Indeed, this is one of the more glorious freedoms—hell, honors, even—of living in Eastern Europe. You can leave work, grab a cold one at the market, and drink it on the walk home. What a country.

Don't feel like paying that speeding ticket in court? Ask the cop if you can "pay the fine now"—hint-hint. Chances are good he'll accept the bribe. I was never refused.

Need a medication but don't feel like making an appointment with a doctor? Just go to the pharmacy. Many drugs, even powerful ones, can be had without any prescription.

Need a break from driving? Just stop anywhere, even in the middle of the street. Drivers park there to check under the hood or just have a smoke, even when there's a perfectly good shoulder right next to them.

Finished with that candy bar? Drop the wrapper on the ground. Don't feel like taking the garbage to the dumpster? Just throw it out your apartment window. That's why they have street sweepers.

Got something stuck in your throat? Hock a good one and let it fly! Even that old lady's doing it on the street. It's like the Old West, without all the tumble weeds.

Hit another car, but there's no serious damage? Just keep driving. I've been in taxis that scrape vehicles, give the other guy a wave and an "Eh," and keep on going.

No tables open at your favorite restaurant? Sit wherever you please. If there's an empty seat at a table, even a table that's occupied, most will let you join their party. The table is not someone's "territory" just because they happened to get there first. "It's a free country!"

And don't feel like leaving the restaurant, even after you've finished eating? Stay as long as you want. I've never, not once, ever, had a waiter bring me the check before I asked for it. You can, almost literally, stay in a Bulgarian restaurant forever. Unlike American establishments, they don't cycle patrons on a conveyer belt with a fixed number of tables that have to turn over. The waiter will never bother you, give you a dirty look, or that annoying leading question, "So . . . anything else for you tonight?" Even if it's closing time, they will usually wait until all the people leave before they actually close, not vice versa.

And, for that matter, they also won't ask you every five minutes, like you're five years old, "How's everything taste? You didn't finish your sandwich? You didn't like it?" (Indeed, you usually have the opposite problem—actually tracking down the waiter to bring you something.)

Bulgaria treats you like an adult, whether you're ready or not.

When I was a resident, the Sofia train station was a microcosm of the country and a good place to watch this freedom in action. Every type of commerce took place there. It was positively medieval. Sellers had all kinds of products from around the world, both real and counterfeit, including food, drink, clothes, accessories, watches, luggage, CDs and videos. There were prostitutes and beggars. Gypsy pickpockets. Boys holding puppies and kittens for sale, though there were free strays everywhere.

And it was all unsupervised. I never saw police in the station. You could come and go, buy and sell, at all hours.

In the beginning, while just visiting Sofia, I slept there on occasion to save a few bucks. For me, it was "the cheapest hotel room in the city."

One time, late at night, I watched a man flash a large kitchen knife, while moving from person to person in the waiting hall. At first, I thought someone should call the police. But it soon became clear that he was just trying to sell the knife to make a quick buck. I imagined him threatening his potential customers with the sales pitch: "Buy this knife or I'll kill you!"

This kind of freedom had a powerful effect on Americans in Sofia. You could see it on their faces and in their changing demeanors. They practically screamed, "I had no idea what was missing in my life!" And "I didn't know I could live like this!" It exhilarated some, scared others. It broke up twenty-year marriages. Indeed, some that came only for a visit ended up quitting their jobs back home, trading in their plane tickets, and staying in Bulgaria.

Obviously, too much freedom has its drawbacks. Sometimes it can be scary and dangerous, especially when it's flirting with anarchy.

There are moments when you want, are even desperate for, that good old-fashioned Anglo-Saxon tradition of following the rules. Like when you're on a plane thirty thousand feet in the air. That's one moment when you hope the pilot is doing what he should be doing, and not just what he feels like doing.

Fortunately, on my own personal nightmare flight, it was only the guys on the ground who took freedom to a new level.

I remember it like it was yesterday . . .

As we touched down at Sofia Airport, smoke started to come out of the right side of the plane. "Daddy, Daddy, we're on fire!" cried the English boy in my row.

I looked out the window. We were on fire alright, or at least, one of the wheels was.

Panic filled the passengers who could see out the window. Some started to cross themselves. There are no atheists on Bulgarian Airlines flights.

We finally came to a stop at the end of the runway. There wasn't a peep from the pilot, no instructions from the stewardess.

A quick-witted passenger filled the silence. "The flight was fine. It was the landing that seemed a little tricky."

And we were not evacuated. We just sat in our seats, wondering what would happen next. Would the fire spread? Would the plane blow up? Was it too late to get another drink?

We watched a crack squad of "firefighters" arrive and assess the problem. And by "firefighters," I mean a handful of overweight, old men in dirty, white t-shirts who stood around, looked at the smoky wing, and pointed.

They all had cigarettes in their mouths.

Eventually, someone squirted a little water on the tire.

Having seen the movie *Airplane* a few hundred times, I wondered what the stewardess would say when we finally deplaned.

To give me something to tell my grandchildren, she did, indeed, thank us for choosing Bulgarian Airlines and hoped we would fly with them again soon. No mention of the fiery landing.

So there are good and bad sides to both philosophies on freedom. In this account, I take the raw definition and note the apparent disparity between it and our American reality.

There is, of course, a happy medium between the two extremes, but who's looking for it? Instead, both sides take their versions too far.

For example, most Bulgarians don't like trash on the street and under their apartment blocks. But, by the time communism collapsed, they had already lost a certain amount of civility and respect for communal property. Indeed, this apparent hyper-personal empowerment has obviously more to do with a decay in society, than a deliberate policy to liberate the people.

As already noted, Bulgaria, in recent years, has joined the postmodern, Western world of the EU and is slowly being sucked into its vortex. Brussels has tried to take away some of its "freedoms," such as smoking pretty much anywhere. Given the ambivalent feelings towards the "new boss," however, Bulgarians are in no hurry to toe the line. Their old habits will surely die hard.

Ironically, these attempted changes are happening before Bulgaria has even reached the modern world. As a result, they are leapfrogging the fun, "middle-aged" years, when they would have had some money and the chance to do the things they dreamed of as a kid. Now, Bulgaria is headed straight to the boring, over-controlled and hyper-sensitive world of old age.

No matter what happens, I doubt they'll ever stop you from buying a large soda.

Chapter Ten

Cairo Makes You Crazy

Egypt

All strange and terrible events we welcome, but comforts we
despise.
—Cleopatra

The "Welcome in Egypt" (sic) sign at the airport should be replaced with the notice, "Cairo makes you crazy. Good luck."

Most tourists would never understand such a warning, however.

After all, Egypt is one of the best places to visit. Hall of Fame.
Top ten in the world. The Pyramids, the Red Sea, the Nile River—
all must be seen at some point in your life. But a short visit is all
you need, one or two weeks, tops. After that, the novelty wears off
and the "mystery" of Egypt has been solved. And you begin to
understand why God chose this place for the plagues.

Most tourists do, indeed, stay for just a short time. They're the
lucky ones.

When I arrived in Egypt, someone gave me the following warning: "Egypt is a great place to visit. But it's very different to live
here." "No kidding," I thought sarcastically. I'd lived overseas. It
couldn't be as bad as he was implying. But this apparently obvious
comment stuck in my head for the rest of my three-year tour.

Let me explain in a long and drawn out way.

Travelers and tourists are short-term, temporary visitors. That is their very nature. They have a start and end date, a reservation at a local hotel, and a departure ticket. They not only know they're leaving, they know when they're leaving. And it's soon. So "even if it's bad, I can endure the rest of the trip standing on my head." They've got it made.

As a result, there is no real attachment—physical, social, professional—to the country. They typically see only the good sides within their "guest bubble." So being a tourist is like just "licking the frosting off the cake."

As a tourist, most of the locals you deal with have been paid to serve you. This leads to you thinking things like, "They seem like such wonderful people. They smile all the time. They're so happy. They really like me. They really like Americans. This is such a warm and friendly country. All is right with the world!"

(By the way, when tourists reciprocate with similar phony smiles and overly-generous tipping, they ruin the lives of expats in countries like Egypt. For when locals now see a foreigner, they expect her to be a rich, grinning-type who throws money to everyone she meets. Indeed, a white face, in many parts of the world, is considered to be like a mobile ATM. Locals think, ironically, as the tourists do of them, "These foreigners are such wonderful people. They smile all the time. They really like me. They must really want to help me!" And when you don't do all these things, you become like an ogre invading the country.)

As a result of this special treatment, the quirks and inconsistencies and downright bizarre—"Oh my God, that guy's driving on the sidewalk"—behavior seems somehow less crazy. It's eccentric, funny even. You can laugh it off. After all, you don't live here. You're leaving soon. And taking nothing with you. Remember that plane ticket?

A place is "exotic" when you're going home soon. It's "madness" when you have to live there.

Living in a country like Egypt, you too can "lick the frosting." Eventually, however, you're also showed exactly how the frosting is made and you decide never to go near another birthday cake again.

When you live in a country, even as a foreigner, you become attached to it, a part of it, even. You see the locals up close, how they think, eat, live, love, and hate, day after day. Sometimes, you can't believe we're made up of the same basic matter and inhabit the same planet.

The difference between tourists and expats is dependence. When you live in a country, you likely have a job, which you rely on for income. You rely on a grocery store or a restaurant to give you food in exchange for this income. You rely on a taxi to take you to the job or restaurant. You rely on the power company to turn on the lights in your apartment. You have a stake in things working right and feel the effects more closely when they don't.

You could, of course, always leave, just like a tourist. But you're less likely to do this when you have responsibilities. Your life is in the country. You'd just have to find another job in another (possibly worse) country. Indeed, I used to motivate myself to stay in Cairo by asking, "What's the only thing worse than having to stay in Egypt? Not being able to stay in Egypt."

But as a tourist, you can just go to the front desk and all will be made well. They will provide you food, security, transportation, or fix your electricity and hot water, all at the drop of a hat. It's a one-stop shop. You rely on the locals, but the reliance is focused on one or two people. People whose livelihoods depend on keeping you happy. It is their full-time jobs to prevent scary reality from creeping into your world.

That's why I've always been jealous of tourists. In Egypt, I became resentful when I saw their bags being loaded into a taxi bound for the airport. In just a few hours, I imagined, they will be home in their normal country, seeing their normal friends, eating their normal food. And they won't have to worry about whether they'll get sick the next day.

As an expat, nothing is prearranged in a package tour. There is no bellman or concierge to find something or take care of you. The line between you and reality is much thinner, often non-existent. In some ways, there is no line. Or the locals see the line, choose to ignore it, and then cross the line.

Most of these observations are pretty obvious. It's the reality of everyday life in the Third World. The difference, in Egypt, is merely the severity of the madness.

At its worst, I thought Cairo was not only mad, but cursed. That "Murphy" guy lived somewhere downtown. Everything seemed to go wrong, all the time, like the city was built on an ancient Indian burial ground.

The madness gets to nearly everyone, eventually. The tourist usually flies away before it can reach her. The expat, however, is not so lucky.

The natural response is, "Why does Cairo make you crazy?" I usually answer this question with a question. "How could you not become crazy after living here?"

When you look at its vital statistics, madness is the only possible diagnosis.

There are almost ninety million Egyptians. The country is the size of Texas and New Mexico combined, but it has three times more people. And according to some forecasters, it will double by 2050.

This fact is even more dramatic when you learn that this many Egyptians are crammed into only five percent of the land, largely along the Nile River and Mediterranean coast. The rest of the space is uninhabitable desert.

Cairo is a megalopolis of twenty million, one of the largest cities in the world, spreading out along the Nile like a thick, brown blanket.

There are apartment buildings as far as the eye can see. Hundreds and thousands of them. From the air, they look like old tombstones sticking up in a massive, over-crowded cemetery.

Egypt is the sixth most-polluted country in the world. The air in Cairo is twenty-times dirtier than the acceptable daily level.

Millions of cars, most too old for emissions controls, spew their toxins every day. Los Angeles may complain about its traffic, but every day is "Carmageddon" in Cairo.

But there are many sources of the dirty air—from burning trash, to suburban factories, to farmers torching their fields to make way for new crops. And the lack of rain helps keep the pollution in place. When you drive into Cairo, the air is so dirty, it often looks like a storm is perched over the city.

You know it's gotten bad when you can not only smell, but taste the air.

The cars, of course, are also a source of noise pollution, a constant, nerve-racking commotion, which provides the "background music" to the bedlam of the city.

Those who call New York the "city that never sleeps" never made it to Cairo. The Egyptians could put even Gotham to shame.

The darkness makes no difference. Midnight is basically the same as, say, 6 pm. The roads, cafes, and restaurants are full at all times of day and night. You see old men playing backgammon in the street at two in the morning like it was two in the afternoon.

The airport is open all night. In fact, three o'clock in the morning is one of the more popular times to fly out of the country.

I'm not sure Egyptians actually ever sleep—not at night, anyway.

Perhaps that's due to the fact that when they finally make it home at the end of the day, they have a depressing scene waiting for them. Most are packed into small, concrete apartments. There is little privacy or room to stretch out or let off steam. There is always another person nearby.

Blackouts are common in the summer when temperatures reach one hundred degrees. Most, however, can't afford air conditioning anyway, so they sleep on the roof of their building.

Egyptian youth probably have it the worst. They do not have a bright future. And most of the population is under twenty-five.

Outside, there are few places for kids to run and play. The majority do not get a good education. Even dating is frowned upon by conservatives and arranged marriages are still common, often to their close relatives. Shudder.

Chances are these youth will also not get a good job. Housing is expensive and hard to find, so they will live with their parents, even after marriage. Most Egyptians earn just a few dollars a day.

They are trapped in their own country. It's difficult to get visas to travel overseas. They are surrounded by miles of sandy desert in every direction.

It seems like the country's greatest days are behind it. Indeed, like others in the neighborhood, they're still riding that whole "ancient empire thing," even though it was thousands of years ago. This phenomenon made me wonder why, if the people have been around for that long, they still can't figure out a good way to run the place?

But I digress. Back to Cairo.

It's difficult for most Egyptians to unwind or escape their hardships, even briefly. There are few parks or trees, little grass or green space. Even fewer places to run, relax, or hit the refresh button.

Still, Egyptians have gotten good at making the best of their surroundings. They eat, play, and relax in the street or in the middle of the sidewalk. Where else are they going to go? The city is basically one big slab of concrete. So they will plop down nearly anywhere, have a seat, and carve out their own little slice of Cairo. Egyptians never met a chair they didn't like.

Others find it harder to adjust to their surroundings.

I met one tourist from Washington, DC, who wasn't able to leave before madness hit her. She had been traveling in the country for two weeks. A female, by herself—not a good combination in a country like Egypt. But she had seen all the brochures that made it seem like a warm and friendly place. Instead, she was harassed, harangued, hissed at, and ogled by Egyptians in every place she went. By the time she was on her way out, she could only describe the country and its people with profanity-laced adjectives.

Each time I arrived in Egypt, I started gritting my teeth, clenching my fists, and bracing myself for the madness that was waiting for me.

The country raises your blood pressure to extraordinary levels. It takes years off your life. Simply being in Egypt is unhealthy.

Why? Well, in addition to the ogling and hissing, nothing is open or honest or upfront. There is no expectation of fair play. Everyone's on the take, the make, trying to survive, to squeeze out one more penny, get some kind of advantage over others. As a result, Egyptians are the most helpful and the most irritating people in the world. A strange paradox.

On the surface, they seem calm, but they can snap like someone flipped a light switch. Because, inside, everyone's on edge, at their wits' end, on a short fuse. It's not a matter of if, but when, they will finally blow. Crowds, traffic, honking, yelling, stress, dirty air, garbage, engines revving . . . cars, cars, everywhere! They come from every direction. Many don't even use their headlights at night because they annoy the drivers in front of them.

A friend was once stopped at a red light, and the driver ahead got out of his car, walked back to his window, and yelled at him because his headlights were shining in his mirror.

This same friend, unfortunately, succumbed to the madness himself. On his commute home from work, he would pull alongside cars that had stopped in an open lane—a relatively common practice—and yell at them in Arabic, "Thank you! Thank you, Einstein!" Perhaps it was cathartic for him. Meanwhile, the Egyptian drivers, not understanding sarcasm, would glance at him, confused, and sometimes wave back, as if to say, "Uh, you're welcome . . . ?"

Cars, cars, and more cars. And when they run into each other—look out! Because Egyptians happen to be the only people in the world who are actually always right—accidents are never their fault. As a result, determining the guilty party can be tricky. So Egyptians skip the usual formalities and go nuclear right away. After all, why wait? The outcome is inevitable. Nearly every accident I witnessed changed from cars hitting each other into people doing the same. Under these conditions, maybe a fistfight's the only real way to determine who's to blame. It's probably a good thing they don't have the bomb.

(Other, apparently untested, theories were shared among expats to explain why so many Cairenes may be crazy. One theory blames high levels of chlorine—a poison—in the tap water. You see, while the Nile is the life-blood of Egypt, the river itself goes through a helluva lot before it gets here, making its way from the bowels of Central and East Africa, through the Sudan, to its last stop before plopping into the Mediterranean. Along the way, you can imagine—or maybe it's better not to try—all the junk that's thrown or emptied into the Nile while it makes its excruciating journey. The river's like a giant test tube for every germ, bacteria, virus, and disease known, and unknown, to man. As a result, it takes quite a bit of chemicals to kill all the alien life forms present in the water before it reaches your tap. Indeed, the water is so chlorinated, bathrooms smell like swimming pools when the faucet's turned on.)

I have a hard time remembering one person in Egypt who was able to prove that he was sane in my book. Most of them are real "drama-daries."

And in case you're wondering—no, my bar was not that high. They just had to have a reasonable amount of, well, sanity. How do I define such a quality? Maybe, to paraphrase a former Supreme Court Justice describing his threshold for obscenity, "You just know it when you see it," and even more so, in the case of sanity, when you don't.

Oh sure, some made a good first impression, but they couldn't keep the madness buried forever. Although more reluctant to let foreigners see them in this way, most Egyptians eventually took that (short) trip to "crazy town," showing their irrational, unreasonable, "I'm never wrong," "It's all about me," "I'm just a little pharaoh" sides. Our last landlords were like this, though we saw no hint of it at the beginning. (The first two landlords were bonkers too, but they let us know that up front.)

At first, they seemed like a charming, even sophisticated, older couple. My wife and I were actually excited. Had we finally met some Egyptians who broke the mold?

This feeling lasted just a few days.

After we moved in, they started to change. They became worried, obsessed, even paranoid, about the apartment, wanting constant updates on its condition. Maybe the problem was that we were now officially on their territory. Little issues became international incidents. They were afraid we were scratching the already-scratched-up hardwood floors. That we'd have loud parties and disturb the neighbors. That we would break the appliances.

We eventually sealed our fate by bringing Chester home. Our building porter immediately ratted us out to the landlady. The latter did not approve of the new addition, even though there was nothing in the lease which said we couldn't have a dog. She tried to convince us to give him back. When that didn't work, she became terrified that the harmless dog was leading to the decline and fall of her precious apartment.

There are those Egyptians who are openly crazy and don't try to hide it. They are comfortable with their madness and almost enjoy the crazies.

Then there are the quietly crazy. They hide it, suppress it, and bottle it up, until one day the cage can't hold them any longer. God help you if you step in front of them that day.

But for me, the worst part of life in Egypt was the presumptions, the tendency of the locals to cross limits and boundaries without asking. Presumptions are the opposite of civilization. If the one word that defines civilization is "No," then a presumption is an unabashed "Yes" to every impulse out there.

"No." As in, "No, you can't stare, whistle, and even make kissy sounds at my wife—while I am holding her hand." Indeed, pity the poor Egyptian women who have to endure even worse harassment every single day. It's such a hostile environment, I imagine even Gloria Steinem would be daunted by the place.

At their worst, much of what Egyptians did on a daily basis would get them shot in the US. Indeed, if this were a novel about the country, there would be few sympathetic characters.

Eventually, all the inner Egyptian stresses and strains, the source of the madness, reached a societal boiling point. Potential energy turned into kinetic, and a mad Molotov cocktail exploded in January 2011 in the so-called "Egyptian Revolution"—a byproduct of the Arab Spring next door in Tunisia. At this point, the condition had reached a new level. It was madness on steroids. The whole country had officially lost its mind.

It had taken years, but it was finally official—Cairo had made its citizens crazy.

My wife and I lived through most of the revolution. For us, the whole thing started on the tennis court. We had just finished a match and were departing, when white smoky tear gas started to float through the air. In hindsight, it was the start of something big, but at the time, it seemed like just another temporary bout of civil unrest. While leaving, we saw security guards donning gas masks and others, without them, with juices flooding from their eyes and noses. They warned us that the demonstrations appeared serious and we should stay for the time being. Since we lived around the corner, we ignored them and walked home, but at a slightly brisker pace due to the tear gas. Their warning turned out to be an omen.

From then on, each day brought something new, some new problem and protest. And it wasn't just about regime change. Everyone had a beef about something. Students protested teachers. Teachers protested students. Civil servants wanted higher salaries. Women (finally!) got their say about harassment. Everyone was angry. There was no normality, no calm, no peace of mind for months at a time. And no apparent end. The Egyptians seemed to be following Trotsky's belief in "permanent revolution."

Anything could set them off. It seemed a few were angry the sun came up every day.

We soon learned that this is a fundamental part of Egyptian culture. Unlike the West, they don't try to change minds by presenting a more compelling argument. They simply wear their opponents down until they finally agree to their demands. In that sense, Egyptians are like a little kid who asks for a cookie, then proceeds to yell and scream incessantly until his mother finally gives in to shut him up.

So it was in the case of the Egyptian Revolution.

Lucky us. We lived close to Tahrir Square and the unpopular Syrian embassy, so we saw, heard, and felt most the "festivities" that came with the revolution. Protests were a daily event. When bad, they turned into running street battles, complete with Molotov cocktails below our apartment. We knew it would be a busy night when that sickly-sweet smell filled the air. We swallowed our share of tear gas, nearly became immune to the stuff, and saw many casualties. We watched with shame as "protesters" scaled the walls of the US embassy and replaced our flag.

The revolution was like a bomb that exploded, was relit, and exploded again the next day. Little, if anything, was done to remove the contents causing the bomb to go off. And the fires that resulted were never fully extinguished, just tamped down for the time being. The roots of the problem, the issues discussed earlier, were rarely addressed, and the tough decisions were put off for another day.

To me, the most bizarre part of the revolution—or perhaps any conflict, really—was the normality of everyday life that existed despite it. (Or, perhaps, it's vice versa.) Commonplace events such as buying groceries felt like asking a stewardess for a soft drink while the plane was crashing. Life continued as before despite the frequent interruptions—daily, sometimes hourly—by angry people doing destructive things, like torching a building or rioting at a soccer match.

Let's look a little closer at buying those groceries. Sometimes your route to the store was blocked by protesters and police. The roads were closed or, perhaps, the store itself was under attack. So you found another place that was open and peaceful to grab some milk and eggs. Coming home, you got out of a taxi and ran into your building because the police were shooting teargas on the street at a mob of angry Egyptians. You didn't get inside quick enough, however, so fluids began to pour from every orifice on your face as you rode up in the elevator. You walked in the door, wiped your face, and unpacked the groceries.

Some wealthy Egyptians rode out the entire revolution at the Gezira Sporting Club, not far from the action downtown. Within the facility, they played golf, swam, and ate nice meals, while fighting raged in the streets nearby.

My wife and I escaped in other ways. When asked what the revolution was like, she often says, "We played a lot of Scrabble and drank a lot of scotch."

Perhaps my biggest lesson was just learning to laugh at the madness. After all, once you lose your sense of humor, especially in a crisis, you're done.

Who can blame the Egyptians for going nuts?

No normal person could live like they did, day in and day out, and stay normal. And crazy people will only become crazier. All the excruciating forces combined to make life so unbearable that madness—or even "revolution"—became the only reasonable outcome.

If someone asked me to diagnose the country's problems and put them into a single, over-simplified analysis, I'd place my hands on the side of my head and yell, "Too many people!"

I mean, come on. They live in the middle of the desert, a place that was never meant to hold people, let alone millions of them.

The Egyptians, of course, are smart enough to know all this, but they don't care. They have a plan. In their minds, a large population insures their relevancy and even dominance in the Middle East. Not possessing any significant natural resources, population size, at some point in time, became a strategic part of their national security. If Egypt only had a few million people, no one would pay much attention. It would merely have the visibility of a country like, say, Oman. But with ninety million people and, perhaps more importantly, an army proportional to its population size, they remain players in the Middle Eastern poker game, flexing their regional power.

Indeed, if you're thinking about starting your own country someday, here are some takeaways from this case study:

Don't put your country in the middle of the desert.

Don't let your people marry their cousins.

Don't prevent your people from drinking.

Don't prevent your people from dating.

Don't allow sidewalk parking. Or, for that matter, any kind of sidewalk sitting, standing, sleeping, storing, or selling. Emphasize the "walk" part of the word.

Do make sure your people can breathe without a gas mask.

Do make sure your country has grass or some other kind of green stuff.

Do make sure you've got some natural resources to sustain yourself, such as oil, gas, coal, trees, farmland, fresh water, fresh air—anything that would justify starting that country in the first place.

Unfortunately for Egypt, there's no going back and no starting over. The country's got to make the best of what it has. Still, it seems like little will ever change. The madness will continue.

Oh, well. Just be glad you're leaving soon.

Chapter Eleven

The Other White Meat

Turkey

If you scratch a cynic, you'll find a disappointed idealist.
— George Carlin

And we did leave soon. Briefly, anyway.

A few months after arriving in Egypt, we evacuated Egypt. The so-called "Arab Spring" had started, and the Egyptians wanted in on the action. It was probably time for a vacation, anyway.

So Egypt had a revolution. When protesters started burning buildings and setting up civilian checkpoints, it quickly became unclear who, if anyone, was really in charge. We were told to "Get out of Dodge" and my wife and I made a break for the airport in order to evacuate.

Playing on the double meaning of the verb, a friend used to say the following about fleeing civil unrest: "First you evacuate, then you leave the country."

At Cairo Airport, we were initially told that the US government-chartered plane would go to Greece. Everyone was excited by the announcement. No country sounded better. By sunset, we would be sitting in a bar on the Mediterranean. We would turn the evacuation into an "evacu-cation."

But it wasn't meant to be.

While waiting to take off, the pilot said that plans had changed, and we were now going to Turkey. This seemed like just another word for "Egypt." A collective sigh of relief turned into a moan of despair. After weeks of revolutionary chaos, Turkey was the last place anyone wanted to go.

On the surface, Turkey looks familiar. Istanbul has cobblestone streets and charming cafes. You spot well-known restaurants. The hotels and shops seem friendly, even Western, with a touch of Eastern flair. There is even historic precedent to this feeling. The city's most famous mosque, now a museum, was once an Orthodox cathedral.

You look at the Turks and think they are just like you. Most wear Western clothes. Some speak English. They even smile now and then.

But then you walk a bit farther and go around the corner.

You see a minaret. You hear the call to prayer. Its feels like you took a wrong turn. Like outsiders have taken over a European country. Or a German and an Arab had a metaphoric love-child, though it was shunned by both sides of the family.

Turkey's on the border between Asia and Europe. It's not quite Arab or Persian, but also not European.

Most of the country's in Asia, with a tiny little chunk jutting out into the "country club" of Europe. And it's trying to get the whole family in on this little "ticket."

The EU's not sure the ticket's "valid," however, and continues to stall Turkey's application, hoping it'll eventually get tired and stop trying to join the club.

What the EU forgets is that in Turkey's part of the world, people don't take rejection well. Somehow, someway, you will pay if you piss them off.

So in revenge, the Turks seem to say, "If the EU doesn't want us on its turf, how would it like millions of people even worse off than we are?" Welcome to the masses. Turkey allows much of the Middle East to enter visa-free. And they've flooded in. Few Iranians or Tunisians want to stay in Turkey. Instead, they use the country as a stepping stone to Western Europe. From Turkey, it's a short hop to Greece or Bulgaria and then onward to Germany and Sweden. Millions have done it over the last decade. Turkey's been more than happy to pocket the transit money they leave behind, while egging the country club that said they were not good enough to join.

This route has only become more popular since the Syrian civil war. Only in the case of Syria, many refugees choose to stay in Turkey, closer to home, while waiting out the war. In this case, the country deserves special recognition for sheltering large numbers of Syrians.

I arrived in Turkey with a suitcase-load of conflicting expectations. On the one hand, I thought that *Midnight Express* was more of a public service announcement, than a Hollywood movie. I didn't expect many good things from the country. Then again, I had heard from everyone who'd been how much they loved Turkey. So I tried to keep my hopes high.

But I soon learned that the worst part about visiting Turkey is the disappointment.

As everyone knows, disappointment is the difference between expectations and reality. And, in reality, I wouldn't have been so disappointed if, before arriving, everyone hadn't told me how great Turkey was. And if, after arriving, the experience had been just a little bit better.

This will sound unfair, but, to me, Turkey is one of the most over-rated countries in the world. And so maybe the blame lies more with those who created those expectations, than with the country itself. Never have so many been so sure a country was so great only to be so wrong. My ultimate Turkish emotion? "Meh."

Don't get me wrong, Turkey's okay. It's not horrific. But it's also not great. Certainly not close to its reputation.

So what does it have going for it? Some interesting architecture, some cool history. Some rocky beaches. Just like its neighbors.

The people were fine. No one was especially friendly or especially mean, except maybe those merchants when they, first, try to sell something and, then, are told, "No thanks."

The food's okay, especially if you're shooting for higher cholesterol. Most of it uses just a few of the same ingredients. One thing's for sure, they love their slabs of meat. Turkish food's like a new take on the scene from *The Blues Brothers* when the boys ask what kind of music the country bar usually plays. Only, this time, the waitress is Turkish and answers, "Oh, we got both kinds a dishes—we got kabobs and rice. And rice and kabobs."

Indeed, it's ironic that the country shares its name with a low-fat, relatively healthy, meat choice. Whoever came up with the name never sampled the cuisine.

Then again, maybe the whole name thing's part of a disinformation campaign to make tourists think that going to Turkey is better for you than it really is. It could all be one giant conspiracy against overweight folks.

Let's look again at those strong recommendations for the country. Many of those who claim to love Turkey are Europhiles. They're used to traveling around the continent, which is relatively safe and predictable. So when they go out of their comfort zone, even just a little, to a country like Turkey, they brace themselves for the worst. After all, it's Muslim! It's the Third World! They're crossing over into Asia. Perhaps it's their first journey to The Other Side. I mean, the national sport is wrestling. Did I mention *Midnight Express*?

But, ultimately, most of the tourists aren't eaten by the locals. They don't get lubed up by any wrestlers—against their will, anyway. In fact, they even meet a few nice Turks. Locals are legendary for being friendly and helpful. What Third World resident wouldn't help you find their shop right away? They're more than happy to help you take that money right out of your wallet.

Like the rest of the Middle East, Turks sell stuff. Stuff like shoes, purses, and those slabs of brown, greasy meat. To help sell those things, they're desperate to find a connection with you and the great U S of A. So they say things like, "Oh, you're from America? My uncle lives in Chicago." In other words, "See, I don't just love sheep. I'm almost like you. I am 'civilized-in-law.'" At these times, I wanted to respond, "Oh, is there a kebab shop in Chicago?"

So these Europhile travelers, when they leave, let out a huge sigh of relief and proclaim the greatness of the country. Turkey is the best! "The best, Jerry!"

It wasn't the outcome that was really that great. It was the difference between the expectations and the outcome.

In the beginning of the evacu-cation, I made an effort to love the country. I wandered throughout Istanbul, meeting many "young Turks" and learning about their lives. They talked about their homeland and often concluded with, "See, we're just like Europe." "Mmm . . . Not really," I thought to myself. "Not that there's anything wrong with that. It's just apples and oranges."

For me, the country wasn't disturbing, it was just too different— from Europe, from Arabia, and, perhaps most importantly, from what I was led to expect.

What is Turkey then? I have no idea. It puzzled me. It tried hard to be familiar but, in the end, was a strange, mixed-up place.

Perhaps this feeling was best illustrated in a simple experience.

Once, while eating out, I had finished my meal and was ready to leave. I looked at the waitress across the room and pretended to write with a pen in the air. And for the first time in my life, the waitress didn't bring me the check. She brought me a pen.

Chapter Twelve

Paradise Lost

Algeria

If the present world go astray, the cause is in you, in you it is to be sought.
—Dante Alighieri

Algeria, to the French, is like an old girlfriend you loved when you were young, the memory of whom you still sigh about in quiet moments. Only now, she weighs three hundred pounds, lives in an abusive household, and has a handful of little rug rats. And she knocks on your door every other day, threatening to kill you for ruining her life.

After being in Algeria, I could see what the French loved about her. She truly seems to have everything a man could want.

First, there are the best of both "hot" and "cold" worlds. Algeria boasts beaches and deserts, mountains and ski resorts. The country is blessed with abundant natural resources. The cities are full of souks, exotic women, and captivating architecture. As the largest country in Africa, its horizons seem to go on forever.

That's why the French fell in love with Algeria. They had to have her. So they invaded and stayed for over a hundred years. Until they were forced out, of course, kicking and screaming.

It was a bad breakup.

After a long, bloody war, the Algerians finally became independent in 1962. They were now free to govern themselves, to live however they wanted. Their future was bright.

But the euphoria ended rather quickly. The country has become the poster child for the reminder "be careful what you wish for."

Algeria, like most post-colonial countries, was like a teenager demanding his freedom from his parents, only to realize his helplessness when they finally grant it. In the end, he struggles to take care of himself and soon goes on food stamps.

Almost a million Europeans fled Algeria after independence. Many of them had helped run the country. And in their haste to skedaddle, they forget to tell the Algerians how to work the washing machine.

Thus, most of Algeria's resulting problems were man-made.

For example, while there's plenty of room in the country, almost ninety percent of it is desert. Compared to Egypt, of course, it's a regular rainforest. But in the case of Algeria, ninety percent of the people are squeezed onto about ten percent of the land. They live on the "green" fringe along the Mediterranean in an otherwise "brown" country.

Algeria, like Egypt, didn't want its natural limitations to stop it from wielding the power of a "big kid on the block." So, adopting the "Egyptian model," its governments encouraged families to fill the country—or at least that habitable ten percent of it—with children. In a sense, it's like a four-foot-tall basketball player who tells himself he's good enough to play in the NBA, however, he also takes growth hormones because he's not totally self-deluded. Algeria's population went from about ten million at independence to forty million today. Many parents, especially in rural areas, had eight to ten kids.

Few countries could absorb such a baby boom, especially one still getting used to taking care of itself. While it was rich in natural resources, economically, Algeria was still a relatively poor country.

Eventually, this led to a demographic crisis. There were simply too many people with no place to live.

Algeria has one of the world's highest occupancy rates for housing. This means that lots of people live in the same apartment—ten, sometimes twenty people from an extended family. In these situations, there aren't even enough beds to go around, so they "hot bunk," taking turns sleeping in the beds.

There are also not enough classrooms for the flood of new students. So school days are broken into morning and afternoon shifts.

Without enough jobs, armies of unemployed young people, upon graduation, stand around on street corners for most of the day with nothing to do. They even have a nickname—the "Wall Leaners." Most are desperate to leave the country; many wishing to join millions of their countrymen in France.

And, as these things do, the demographic crisis eventually turned into a political one.

By the late 1980s, the new generation had come of age and wanted to change the military-dominated government. An Islamic party won the first free elections, results of which were then canceled by the army. A terrorist insurgency (or civil war, depending on your perspective) broke out soon afterwards. Attempting to sow chaos in the country, armed groups massacred civilians in droves, butchering, mutilating, and at times, wiping out entire villages. It was pure savagery, death on an apocalyptic scale. Over the last two decades, hundreds of thousands of people have died.

I read local newspapers every day. There were only a few mornings when I didn't see notice of a reported terrorist attack someplace in the country.

In the West, after just one attack, people lose their minds. Imagine if these were daily events—ambushes, bombings, beheadings, fake checkpoints, disembowelments.

When it happens every day, it becomes part of the landscape. Even abnormal events become almost normal. And vice-versa. An attack-free day becomes abnormal.

As a result, security concerns were paramount for Westerners in the country. Some joked that their main job was to "hold the fort" and "raise the flag" each day.

As a result, many developed "compound fever"—a form of extreme claustrophobia related to "cabin fever," but caused by long periods of confinement. Some joked that the high walls and barbed wire were intended to keep them inside, rather than the others out.

For those locked down, one of the only outlets, or "inlets" in this case, was the Marine Bar on the embassy compound, which was open to visiting Americans. Thursday night was "The Happy Shack," an event hosted by the Marines, during which locals and expats could escape the realities of the war for a few hours. Of course, given the security situation, Algerians had to be "asked and approved" by someone at the embassy before they could come. So an invitation to a Happy Shack—complete with drinks, dancing, music, and other rarities in Muslim Algeria—became a prized commodity. It may have been the hottest ticket in town, perhaps even the whole country.

For many Algerians, "The Shack" was their only chance to meet Americans and let their hair down. Large numbers of teenage "groupies" dressed conservatively when leaving home and entering the embassy, walking past Marines with automatic weapons. But when they got to the bar, they "changed" dramatically—literally and figuratively. They went straight to the bathroom where they applied make-up and shimmied into provocative, short-cut skirts and dresses. The evening was a treat for those on compound, too. Many locals are strikingly beautiful and not a few relationships ended with Americans taking home Algerian brides, which, frankly, was the goal of many Algerians who came to the bar.

Algeria, before 9/11, was one of the most dangerous countries in the world. These days, the conflict has largely fizzled out, although there are still random attacks, especially in the south and east. Indeed, these days, Algeria is relatively benign compared to many of its neighbors, as terrorism and civil war have spread throughout the region.

The country is trying to make a fresh start.

In the meantime, maybe France could learn to love Algeria again. Algeria sure could use his help in getting back on her feet. Both have done lots of growing up. Talk to both sides and you will see they still have feelings for each other. The Algerians want to go to France, while the French reminisce about the way Algeria once was. The relationship would have to be on different terms, however, there may be a future for them. After all, one of those "rug rats" looks a lot like him.

Chapter Thirteen

Taxi!

Egypt

The first thing that strikes a visitor to Paris is a taxi.
—Fred Allen

If Forrest Gump went to Egypt, he'd say that the taxis, too, are "like a box of chocolates," since you never know what you'll get till you get in and go for a ride.

On the outside, they look like any others you've seen around the world—four wheels, a metal frame, and some squiggly writing you probably can't understand. After a while, however, you realize they are not what you are used to.

Taxis are a daily adventure in Egypt.

Most are taxis in name only. There are few professional drivers in Egypt, even if they happen to do the job full-time. More often, they are just a guy in a car who's passing by when you need a ride. I'm not sure whether they have to take any kind of test to get a taxi license. If so, they certainly don't have to pass the test to start driving.

I took hundreds of taxicabs during my time in Cairo. Each had its own story and its own vibe, according to the type of driver and the condition of the vehicle, and vice versa.

Take, for example, the deaf taxi driver. And, yes, in case you wondered, his impairment, initially, only made me yell louder. But it didn't do any good. I had to point out each turn he needed to take. This was a particularly dangerous handicap given that driving is an auditory activity in Egypt. I wondered if I would find a blind driver next.

No, the next one wasn't blind, but he was on his deathbed—eyes glazed and practically drooling on himself. "Now that's dedication," I thought. "Here this guy's about to have a heart attack, maybe even on his way to the hospital, and he's trying to make a few more bucks." Ultimately, we flagged down another Egyptian who made sure he would be okay.

Then there was the "relay driver." This guy, without saying a word, pulled off the road, got out, and was replaced—right then and there—by another driver, like we were in a relay race. At this point, I learned that many Egyptian drivers don't actually own their cars, but merely lease them for a few hours per day. As a result, there can be several relaying the same car. That day, our driver's shift just happened to be over half-way from the airport, so he stopped and punched out.

Lastly, let's not forget the whimsical driver who went swimming with us in the Red Sea. One weekend, my wife and I arranged, in advance, to have a car take us to the Red Sea about two hours away from Cairo. However, when we went to the hotel the next day to pick up our ride, the driver didn't show. Not wanting to waste a Saturday, we simply flagged down a cab and asked if he'd take us to the beach. He didn't hesitate; after all, the money seemed reasonable. He was in! He ferried us to the beach and even jumped in the water until it was time to go home. It was our first all-day taxi ride.

There are two main types of taxis in Egypt—black and white—which is a good indication of the difference between them.

Black taxis are usually old relics from the 1970s. Most don't have meters or, at least, ones that work, so you negotiate the fare, which is usually fair, since you can go miles and miles for practically nothing. Many are Ladas or Dachas from Eastern Europe, bought when Egypt had a special relationship with the Soviet Union. They seem like they belong in a black and white movie. The drivers usually look like old farmers.

The white taxis are newer Korean and Japanese models, with working meters and air conditioning. They charge more per mile, as a result. Some are tricked out with colorful seats and disco lighting, reflecting the driver's own personal style, since he is often sporting tight jeans and an even tighter pink shirt. The tourists and well-to-do choose the white taxis.

Indeed, you can tell a lot about someone by their preference.

I liked the black taxis and took them whenever possible. Each time, I felt like I was striking a blow at pretension, opting for tradition and the little man. The black taxis are definitely old school—old, dirty, and classic. They are what they are, take it or leave it. If your grandpa were an Egyptian taxi driver, he'd be in a black one.

And those who take black taxis are realists. They accept the world as it is and try to embrace it. They don't need to be separated from the dirt and noise of the outside. They become one with the elements.

Those who take white taxis are idealists. They live in the realm of what could or should be. They shun reality and need to be insulated against it. They want their window to the world firmly closed. The outside only disturbs their fantasy.

The main problem with both kinds of taxis is that the drivers aren't up to speed on the little nuances of the job—like the location of streets, shops, restaurants, or, really, anyplace that has an address. Oh sure, they can find the airport, but if you need to go to a non-aviation-related location, you're often out of luck.

I have been half a mile from major streets and intersections with a driver who did not know how to get there. I've been lost in a well-known suburb with a driver who couldn't find his way out. I've had drivers who didn't know how to get to the largest shopping mall in the country.

As a result, Egyptian taxis are almost "self-service." You must know how to get to your destination before you get in the cab. The research is up to you. As a friend used to say, "The place is easy to find, once you know how to get there."

Then you guide the driver along the way, "Left . . . right . . . left . . . right . . . straight—stop! Yes, here. Heeeeere!" For some reason, drivers don't believe you when you tell them to stop. They need confirmation. Sometimes confirmed confirmation.

Obviously, not everyone has nice things to say about Egyptian taxis. There are passengers who've been cheated, robbed, groped, and worse. In this way, they are like bad taxis in every other country on Earth. Some will "take you for a ride" by going the long way to make an extra buck. Some will stop and pick up a "friend," who may then try to harm you. Others may rig the meter to make it run faster, or if the fare wasn't agreed upon in advance, demand an extra-large amount from you.

That said, I took taxis nearly every day for three years and had an astonishingly small number of problems, most of which involved a minor disagreement over the fare. The average driver was completely polite or humbly quiet while doing his job. Indeed, drivers work long hours for little money. The fares are ridiculously low—a dollar or two to go miles and miles. Thank you, subsidized gasoline.

And, if you can communicate with your drivers, some have a good sense of humor. They will joke that the ride is free and that they can't possibly accept payment from someone as wonderful as you!

Chapter Fourteen

Applied History

Romania

It will all be the same after a hundred years.
—Romanian proverb

If Bulgaria was my first love, then Romania was a mistress on the side.

I chose to be with Bulgaria, but I also had strong feelings for her cousin across the Danube River. And I visited her—I mean, it—as much as possible.

They both appealed to me largely for the same reason—visiting them felt like going back in time.

Romania was more progressive than other countries, of course. Indeed, if Afghanistan was like going back to the Stone Age, then Romania was only the Middle Ages. It was a shorter trip back in time.

Having studied medieval history, there was no more exciting journey.

When I arrived in Romania, especially in the countryside, the characters I had learned about in history books suddenly came to life. They leaped off the page and stood right in front of me. They were now in 3-D.

I could see their faces, hear their stories, even touch and talk to them. I could know what it was like to live in the past.

As there is Applied Physics, this was "Applied History."

Still, such words prove somewhat of an oxymoron. After all, history has already happened. You're not supposed to see its face. It should be resting peacefully in books and museums.

As a result, you feel like you're breaking some sort of time code by going to Romania. You're seeing what was meant to have already happened.

And I can't help but stare when I'm in Romania. I am drawn to them like a physicist to an atom bomb.

I love to look in their eyes, see their clothes, hear them talk. They are not like me. They belong in a different century. But they prove that the slow, simple, communal ways you thought were long gone are still alive.

Strangers strike up conversations on trains, share food, and cross themselves before pulling out of the station.

Most Romanians live in villages and small towns. About a third still farm. And they're not modern farmers. Much of the work is done by hand or hoof. They're real and—in my mind—noble peasants.

Romanians cut tall grass with scythes, grow what they eat, ride in horse carts. Animals pull the plows in the fields. Most rural homes still use wells and outhouses.

Who knew Romanians were so Amish?

Despite these relatively primitive conditions, Romania, like Bulgaria, was welcomed into the EU and NATO in recent years.

Makes you wonder if any of the Western government bureaucrats who came up with the strategy to expand these organizations to the Balkans ever actually visited the target countries. Or, if so, whether they ever left their hotels. It wouldn't have taken much. Just a short drive into the countryside and maybe they would've had second thoughts about whether they were really ready to join.

Many hope these bureaucrats will help drag Romania into the modern age.

Apparently, some did visit the train stations. There, you will find fabulous trash cans. How many times in life can you say that?

Each can is divided into four subsections—"paper," "plastic," "glass," and "refuse"—for easier recycling. "It's just like Western Europe," you think. Such a wonderful waste bin must've been the result of an EU program.

Then you go to throw some trash in an appropriate opening. Wait a second! On closer inspection, you see that the dividers don't extend to the bottom of the can. All the items are mixed together within the bin. It's all a ruse, a sham, a crock. It's all for appearances. A real Potemkin trash can.

And here's the best part—the trash can's see-through!

Don't get me wrong. While they might not be "ready for prime time," Romanians are good souls—warm, easy-going, and hospitable. I've hitch-hiked from one end of the country to the other, and back, and never had the smallest problem, other than looks of disbelief that an American would bum rides through their homeland.

And Romanians love America. They want to be our fifty-first state. They joke that they should declare war on the US so that we will defeat them and rebuild their country.

Romania's also a beautiful place. And, unlike the rest of Europe, most of Romania's best sites lie off the tourist track. You won't stand in many lines while visiting its attractions.

But letting the country into exclusive clubs like the EU and NATO is like admitting "Cooter" from *The Dukes of Hazzard* into MIT. You may need him to fill your Appalachian quota, but you're going to spend most of the time explaining to him how the drinking fountain works.

Romania should've been given more time to catch up to the modern age. They'll get there someday, one trash can at a time. I just hope they're not in too big of a hurry.

Chapter Fifteen

And Now for Your International Forecast

Egypt

Everybody talks about the weather, but nobody does anything about it.
—Charles Dudley Warner

Here are a few words that will turn your idea about what the weather is like in other countries upside down and make you reconsider that winter getaway.

It snows in Egypt.

Yep, in the desert. In the middle of the hot, dry, sandy Sahara, where you imagine it's a thousand degrees every day, all year round, and the sun makes your skin melt.

Everyone knows that the desert gets cold at night. But it also, on extremely rare occasions, snows there in the winter. Just flurries, of course, most of which don't even reach the ground. But it's still the white stuff. Trust me. There are photos of a dusting on the Sphinx at Giza in 2013.

Tourists come to Egypt to escape the winter of the northern countries. In fact, for many Third World countries, weather is a valuable commodity. But if Egypt is the destination, what will these snowbirds get?

Cairo boasts fifty or sixty degree temperatures, with nights in the forties. Our apartment heater ran most nights from December to March. Not really tropical temps.

Tourists march off to Red Sea resorts, which are marketed as year-round destinations. I was amazed at how many thought they were going to lie out, play on the beach, and swim in the middle of winter. Indeed, the sun may shine every day in Egypt, as the well-known television commercial claims, but winter still brings on the goosebumps.

Some days on the coast, it's only fifty degrees, windy, and water temperatures are in the sixties or seventies. For a beach resort, that's freezing. Who wants to lie on cold, blowing sand? Perhaps it could be training to join the "Polar Bear Club."

Many tourists spend their winter Egyptian vacation covered up on the beach, only not to shield them from the sun's rays. They wonder why they spent thousands of dollars to travel all this way and still be cold. "At least it's not snowing like back home!" they say. But it could.

In the summer, Cairo gets hot—infernally hot. But it's only like that for a few months each year. And only warm—above eighty degrees—for about half the year. Much of the time, it's either cold, cool, luke-warm, or quite comfortable. Not hot or scorching hot.

When it is hot, it's more like a steam bath than a sauna, since it's not particularly dry heat, even though you're in the desert.

Indeed, it doesn't rain much, but the city's proximity to the Mediterranean and the Nile River Delta keeps humidity hovering between fifty and sixty percent for most of the year, which is on par with Atlanta.

Cairo, then, in the middle of the Sahara desert, is just as humid as green, wet Hotlanta.

For me, however, Cairo was never hot enough.

Don't get me wrong. I didn't love the heat at first. It's a sticky, sweaty swelter when the air barely moves and you move even less. When a thin layer of sweat covers your skin all day long.

All winter, I looked forward to the warmth of summer. Then it arrived, and I was miserable. I somehow missed it when it was gone, but agonized when it finally arrived. After all, it wasn't really warmth, but a suffocating fever, that came with summer. I hated it for weeks. "It's too damn hot!" I'd exclaim. "You can barely breathe!" "Who wants to walk around sweating all day long?"

Gradually, I realized I could never beat the summer, so I chose to join it. We had one air conditioner, and it was in the bedroom. (Like most, sleeping is my one activity wherein the heat can play no part.) The rest of the house stayed hot. So I opened up windows and embraced it. And it reciprocated.

Warmth became a primal emotion. It even, ironically, gave me goosebumps and made my skin tingle. For me, it was a revolutionary concept to never feel even a hint of cold. My version of heaven moved a little closer to hell. In Egypt, I learned that I would rather sweat than shiver. And, if I wasn't sweating, I was too cold.

The heat became a second layer of clothes, surrounding me like a force field. Or, in some ways, the only layer, since I just wore shorts around the house. The moisture on my skin was a familiar friend. It stayed close to me, hugged me, rippling like a warm massage all day long.

As in any relationship, acceptance turned into enjoyment, then to love, then to need and, finally, to addiction and obsession. I couldn't live without the heat. I had to be warm all the time. But every year, she left in the fall, making me despondent. And cold. But we'll always have summer in Cairo.

Indeed, learning to love the heat was the biggest lesson I took from Egypt. Literally, I accepted the heat and let it consume me. Figuratively, I accepted the "heat," or "all the things in a strange place that I couldn't control."

More practically, I make these seemingly trivial points because I've found there is a disconnect between the perception and reality of a country's climate. I think we sometimes assume that if a place seems far away and exotic, its weather must also be proportionally harsh or unfamiliar. So we imagine extreme weather in places with relatively normal conditions for their latitude.

I've been guilty of this many times.

My first was in Spain. After college, I traveled around Europe for a few months, starting in Madrid, the furthest place my parents' frequent flyer miles would get me.

At the time, I thought the Mediterranean was warm and exotic, tropical even, all year-round. After all, they have palm trees and beaches. And the pictures always show people diving off boats and swimming in the water. No one's ever got a coat on.

Turns out, you can only do those things for a few months of the year. Most of the time, the Med's a cold, windy place. The seas are rough and the water freezing.

So I showed up in Spain in March, wearing shorts. That's all I packed. I was ready to start my European trip.

As soon as I stepped off the plane, I started to shiver. It was freezing. Rainy and cold. The palm trees looked confused and out of place. And so did I.

So think twice before you book that Red Sea vacation in February. Egypt, after all, is about the same latitude as the US Gulf Coast. Most people don't spend their winter vacation at the Biloxi beach.

But if it's not what you expect, weather-wise, even in the Sahara, where is it truly always warm?

The Tropics. That's the only place in the world where it's reliably hot and sticky all the time. Even at night, even in January. Indeed, as they say, there are three seasons in a place like tropical Thailand: hot, very hot, and hot and wet.

The tropics. A place, where, when the A/C goes out in the middle of the night, the bugs fly in your sweaty ears, and you wonder if you remembered to take your malaria medicine that day. Of course, the mosquitos could be carrying dengue fever instead.

So you write off sleep for another night.

The tropics it is. That's where you should go for your winter vacation.

At least it won't snow.

Chapter Sixteen

Land of the Limping Dog

Romania

If you pick up a starving dog and make him prosperous, he will not bite you; that is the principal difference between a dog and a man.
—Mark Twain

Romania is a great place to adopt a pet. There are lots of dogs and cats that no one seems to want. You literally have, for lack a better cliché, the pick of the litter.

And you don't have to travel all the way to the animal shelter. Just go out to the street and grab the one you like most. Soon you'll have a new best friend for life.

The army of stray animals is one of the first things you notice when arriving in Romania. They are a permanent yet mobile fixture of the landscape. They are our "silent" friends and neighbors. The animals are also the most depressing part of Eastern Europe. Something that never becomes normal. How do you get used to seeing a little dog shaking in the cold?

The unwanted dogs and cats are one of the products of the end of communism.

Many households believed that, when the economy fell apart, they could no longer afford to take care of their pets, so they opened their front doors and let them out—for good. You can see the results everywhere. Among the strays, there are an inordinate number of curly-haired, formerly pampered lapdogs scavenging for food. They seem sadly out of place. Once they wore little red sweaters; now they eat out of garbage cans. I often wonder how the former owners and dogs would react to each other if they passed on the street.

At the same time, with the breakdown of civil society, the Romanian government was no longer willing or able to handle the new wave of unwanted animals.

So after moving outside, the now-feral dogs and cats stayed there.

Despite this history, or perhaps because of it, Romanians have an ambivalent relationship with the animals.

Some are protective of them. They consider them fellow beings in need of help. Maybe they see in them a little of themselves, creatures trying to survive in a world that's been turned upside down.

While most aren't willing to take them into their homes, some residents leave the front door to their apartment building open so dogs can sleep in the lobby on cold nights. Others build tiny houses outside their buildings. Little old ladies toss them food from their kitchen windows.

And they protest whenever the government announces a new plan to euthanize the animals.

There have also been ridiculous programs designed to help them. One summer, there were a large number of stray dogs with flea collars, the apparent result of an EU plan to keep them pest-free. Many realized the futility of such a project.

To others, however, the animals are living, breathing reminders of their own misery and mistakes that never seem to go away. They take their anger out on them, sometimes even setting out poisoned meat in parks—which often ends up killing peoples' pets.

The chapter title refers, sadly, to the large number of Romanian dogs that have been kicked, beaten, hit by rocks, cars, or been in fights with other dogs. The country resembles a giant VA hospital for animals. One of my saddest Romanian moments occurred when I watched a dog barking furiously at every car that passed by a dead dog lying in the street, seemingly angry at each vehicle for killing his friend.

Meanwhile, the dogs continue to go forth and multiply. There seems to be no reasonable way to solve the problem.

And they are everywhere, from big cities to tiny villages, in parks and under parked cars, in the streets and on the farms.

They roam the cities, looking for food, friends, and safe places. They know where to go for a drink of water, which dumpsters have the best leftovers.

They are both solitary and communal. Some travel alone, others in packs.

I've run into groups of ultra-feral dogs in the countryside—packs of growling, foaming, Satanic strays from Hell. Dogs in name only.

I've seen them get on and off trams and buses in the city, look both ways before crossing the street, cross with humans, and sleep on the front steps of Parliament.

I've seen a litter of puppies living in an unused x-ray machine at the airport.

The dogs are as diverse as us humans. They come in all shapes and sizes, colors and breeds, personalities. Some are pure breeds, others barely look like canines. Some want to play, others to be left alone. Some are healthy, others near the end.

But stray dogs share one common trait—they're all on the bottom rung of society.

They smell. Their hair is ratty. They look like they haven't eaten in days. Some have been traumatized or suffer mental problems. They find strangers for companionship but are always on the lookout for danger or opportunity.

The life of a stray dog is shameful on many levels. Unlike some human conditions, they played no real part in causing their misery. They are a consequence of someone else's bad decisions. Yet they hold almost no grudge. That's one of the best parts of adopting an abused or unwanted animal. They remember where they came from and are forever grateful to the one who saved them.

A few of my American friends adopted dogs or cats off the street to keep as their own. One took a stray dog to a Romanian vet, who, even after a physical exam, concluded that the animal was male, when she was actually female. The friend named the dog "Vincent" in honor of the crack Romanian veterinarian.

What could such an animal possibly think when she's pulled off the street? It must be the same level of drama when she was kicked out of her old house. Only this time, the process is reversed and her life changes for the better. One minute, she's walking down the street, trying to survive another day, dirty, hungry, riddled with fleas. Then a complete stranger grabs her, puts her in his car, and takes her to his big house. Now, she gets two meals a day, fresh water, dog biscuits, baths, and constant attention. She even sleeps in his bed.

One thing's for sure. She's a lucky dog. Maybe a few really do have their day.

Chapter Seventeen

Kramer vs. Kramer

Moldova

Choose your parents carefully.
—Sebastian Coe

Moldova is the only country I've been to which did not have a Coca-Cola bottling plant or a golf course.

At first glance, these things may seem relatively insignificant. But I've found them to be two of the most important items necessary before you officially call yourself a "real country."

Even Burkina Faso has a golf course. Afghanistan has both the Kabul Golf Club and its own Coke bottler.

So maybe Moldova isn't a real country after all. It just plays one on TV. Indeed, ask most people, at least outside of Europe, and they will say you made up the place.

I agree, the name does sound made up. Moldova? Really, that's the best you could come up with? Any country that begins with "mold" is a little strange. How about "Moldistan" or "Land of the Moldmen?" Both sound like cheap horror movies.

When it's used in a company's name, it sounds even weirder. So their mobile phone company is called, you guessed it, Moldcell. Make sure to wash your hands after using the phone. There's Mold-

presa, the state news agency, Moldcargo, for shipping, and Mol-
dindconbank. And don't forget Moldbread, the national bakery.
Okay, I made up that last one.

To be fair, Moldova does have a Coca Cola plant. It's just located in Romania.

That pretty much sums up why Moldova's probably not a real
country—or, at least, its own country, to be more precise. It has
belonged to either Romania or Russia for most of its modern history. And both miss it and want it back.

Moldova is one of those relatively poor, precarious territories
which borders greater powers, but whose status seems unsettled,
largely because those greater powers continue to pine after it. After
all, most lands around the world have already been claimed by
somebody. If there's a place left with even a hint of unresolved
status, others will vie for it. Other states and territories in the same
predicament include the Western Sahara, Afghanistan, and Eastern
Congo.

Moldova is like a child of separated parents Romania and Russia. And its history? One long, international custody battle. The
parents were never formally married, though they lived next door to
each other. Maybe that's another reason why Moldova's an "illegit-
imate country." Since they both want the kid, really bad, the case is
reargued almost every day.

To many, it's puzzling as to why parents would fight so hard for
such a scrawny little kid. Perhaps each merely doesn't want the
other one to have it.

Indeed, bloody wars have been fought for Moldova. Borders
redrawn. Names have been changed to try to confuse others into
thinking they had the "wrong kid." For example, when the Russians
got custody, they called it "Bessarabia." Later, they made it a Soviet Republic. But to the Romanians, it will always belong to their
province Moldavia, aka Moldova.

Romania seeks to accentuate Moldova's Romanian qualities, its "Romanian-ness," if you will, by promoting ideas like "Moldovan history is really just a part of Romanian history," and "The Moldovan language is another name for Romanian." Bucharest hopes this will eventually lead Moldova to rejoin Romania as part of its eastern province.

Russia is afraid that, if this happens, it could lose some of its influence in the region, and that the Russian minority living in the country would then be isolated and ignored. So it supports Moldova in accentuating its "Moldovan-ness," showing the world that the country has its own unique identity. A few years ago, a pro-Russian government in Chisinau even put out its own "Moldovan-language" dictionary, a dictionary that largely resembled a Romanian dictionary, and drew laughs from actual Romanians—I mean, Moldovans.

That was a very Balkan thing to do. Many in southeastern Europe believe that if they call something what they want it to be, it will become that entity. This logic proclaims that it's not possession that's nine-tenths of the law, but rather whose name is on the damn thing.

I had a revealing conversation with a Montenegrin before her country's independence from Yugoslavia. She told me, "At the moment, I speak Serbian." "And what will you speak after independence?" I asked. "Montenegrin, of course." I couldn't help but smile.

But these naming tactics have apparently worked. Most Moldovans are ethnic Romanian, speak what is, for the most part, standard Romanian, and live in lands that were once part of Romania. In surveys, however, a majority consider themselves "Moldovan" and their country to be a sovereign nation, not just a once-and-future-part of Russia or Romania.

After all that fussing, you'd think the place was like Disneyland. But Moldova has an unremarkable landscape—a bland, flat, boot-shaped country on the eastern border of the Balkans. It lies between Europe and the Russian steppe, but neither side can agree on the exact property line.

The country has few people, few resources, no real army, and no real national purpose. There are no mountains or beaches. And, most importantly, not a single golf course. But I already covered that.

The Moldovan government keeps its people on a short leash, as if the KGB still ran the show. Platoons of police march through the capital, Chisinau, providing constant reminders to think twice before stepping out of line.

The message is intended for visitors too. Foreigners are stopped, without cause, by both uniformed and plain clothes police who demand to see their "papers." You can be taken in for questioning if you happen to be without your passport or have over-stayed the time allowed in the country.

The culture has all the excitement and flavor of a loaf of Wonder Bread. National dress? A track suit. Architecture? A drab apartment block. Food? Dull and greasy. Its national dish, *mamaliga*, consists of a cornmeal mush similar to grits.

(Beware, though, because *mamaliga* is the "feats of strength" food for expats in Moldova. Every country has one. Your fortitude will be challenged if you don't proclaim its goodness. To others, loving a food like *mamaliga* is a hint that they've—get ready— "gone native!")

Moldova's kind of like North Dakota opened its own country.

A self-proclaimed cheapskate, I ate in state-run canteens, which were popular for their low-priced dishes. Doing so made me feel like I was in a scene from *One Flew Over the Cuckoo's Nest*. The places were full of pensioners. In winter, you kept your coat and hat on, since they were cold and poorly-lit. The napkins on the table were pulled apart into thin, individual layers and cut into smaller portions to make them go a little further. This practice only made me grab an even bigger handful to get my money's worth and "stick it to the man."

The clientele looked like a group of prisoners or mental patients. We lined up and slid our trays, cafeteria-style, while making our selections. "No talking in line!" said the old, scowling woman behind the counter. Her hair was dyed a deathly orange and she wore a thick coat of bright make up.

Under the glass, there were greasy, flattened fillets of meat called "*batuta*" and bowls of freshly-slaughtered chicken and noodles in hot watery broth called "*zama*." For the health-conscious, there was a rainbow of salads with every possible concoction of incongruous, "left-over" ingredients you could imagine, such as herring, beet, and egg-white-salad or the ever-popular mushroom, olive, and potato glob. Each of these choices were slathered with a thick layer of yummy mayonnaise. (Moldova is a mayo-lover's dream. They even put the stuff on pizza.) Mmm . . . and don't forget a side of *mamaliga*! For dessert, there was a gelatinous, jello-like substance, which looked like it came straight from the abattoir.

In a recent survey of sixty countries, Moldovans came out as the "Unhappiest people in the world." And that bar's got to be pretty high—I mean, low—in such a survey.

I don't blame them. Even the shopping's depressing. The "malls" haven't changed their displays since the 1950s. They are "commie-chic." A Stalin statue would fit in well in the entrance way. You step inside a typical Moldovan mall to endless rows of small, soul-crushing kiosks, each selling the same imported Turkish boots and purses. How's a shopper to decide? Should I get the fake-leather black shoes or the other fake leather black shoes? There are so many of the same to choose from! It's like Henry Ford designed all the products . . . "You can have any color of shoe you want, as long as it's black!"

(As an aside, I will say that I admire the Moldovan attitude toward nudity or, rather, their apparent indifference. At the local gym, the female cleaning lady would often barge into the men's locker room, unannounced, while other patrons were showering or in various stages of undress. No one even blinked as she started mopping the floor around us. If this were America, such a scene would have been the start of a porno movie.)

And don't get me started on the furniture. When my wife and I looked at sprucing up our apartment, we learned that Moldova's the only country where you're not allowed to try the merchandise, before buying. I attempted to sit on a stiff, over-priced sofa and was quickly yelled at—"Hey, get off that!" That's customer service, "Moldovan-style." Marx would've loved the place.

Not that Moldovans have much money to spend anyway, since they're the poorest country in Europe. The average worker makes about three hundred bucks a month. Meanwhile, a select group of former communists and gangsters pillage the country. Many of them live on the appropriately-nicknamed "Mafia Mountain," a place kind of like the Beverly Hills of Chisinau, if Beverly Hills only let in Tony Soprano-types. The so-called "mountain" is a slight misnomer, though, since it looks more like that small hill you used to sled down as a kid. From it, however, you have awe-inspiring views of belching smokestacks and concrete apartment blocks around the capital.

You can also see the *biznesmen's* fancy German cars cruising through town. They stick out when parked next to thirty-year-old, rusty Ladas. The son of a former prime minister who, some think, owns half the city goes around in a shiny new Rolls Royce. Given the surroundings, he might as well drive a spaceship.

The Romanians and Russians want Moldova more than the Moldovans. One quarter of the population has gone abroad. (If a proportional number of people left the US, it would mean losing about eighty million people.) The Moldovan expats work in Western Europe or Russia and send money back to their families. In fact, more than a quarter of Moldovan GDP comes from these remittances. Many more would join them if they could, even though some who left were trafficked as part of the international sex trade.

As if that weren't enough, did I mention Moldova's awfully close to downtown Chernobyl?

When the zombies finally take over the world, they will come from Moldova.

With so much going for them, thank God they love to drink.

Few Moldovans want to stay. Even fewer foreigners want to visit. Tourism is virtually non-existent, apart from a few backpackers collecting unique stamps for their passports. Only a tiny number of expats live in the country. And corruption is—surprise!—the national sport. So there is little foreign investment, other than massive injections of cash from the EU and the US to convince it to stay out of Russia's camp.

Two American businessmen who had opened Western-style restaurants were quickly run out of town when their Moldovan "partners" decided they wanted to keep the places for themselves. They used friends in the government to make doing business nearly impossible, so that the foreigners eventually sold their stakes in the restaurants to the partners for less than they were worth.

This official coercion is applied to local entrepreneurs as well. Whereas in Bulgaria, the mafia used to extort your business, much of the criminal activity in Moldova has been nationalized. So it's not the local gangs you have to fear but such malicious government officials as the friendly neighborhood "health inspector" who certifies that your restaurant is up to code.

The problem is that the code is intentionally made so opaque and arbitrary, owners end up paying a "fine" to the inspectors, knowing that otherwise, the latter will gin up reasons to keep them closed indefinitely, all the while squeezing them for money.

Heads you pay. Tails you close.

So, to recap, you have two major ethnic groups in the country, Romanians and Russians. They don't like each other. Their home countries don't like each other. They don't especially like their home countries. They speak different languages, believe in different versions of history, and have different ethnic heritages—one Latin, one Slavic. One looks West for guidance and identity, the other East. Many have already left, and most would join them if they could. You can imagine what family dinners are like.

It seems logical Moldova should look more West than East. After all, the majority of its population is ethnic Romanian and identifies with the cousins across the Prut River. The government in Bucharest has given Romanian passports to hundreds of thousands of Moldovans to help solidify these bonds. And a future in the EU would likely be better than another Soviet Union.

But nothing in this part of the world is that simple.

If this were a "David-vs.-Goliath" situation, Russia would play Goliath. But Romanian David is too scared to throw rocks at him. He knows that the "little Goliaths" running around Chisinau would give "Big Goliath" in Moscow a call—eventually leaving David dead on the battlefield, squished like a grape.

Although a minority in Moldova these days, the ethnic Russians, when they were known as "Soviets," were in charge of the place. The ethnic Romanians remember all too well what that felt like and don't want to stir that pot. But this fear often keeps Moldova from moving in a Westerly direction—or any direction, for that matter.

So as Lenin used to ask, "What is to be done?" What will happen to Moldova? Who should get the "kid?"

Should they cut it in two, "Solomon-style?" Turn a small, poor country into two smaller, poorer countries?

Russia has helped make the answer even more complicated by taking the custody battle to a whole new level.

For years, Moscow has threatened not to cut Moldova in half, but rather to "slice off its ear." The "ear," the bargaining chip, is the self-styled "Transnistrian Republic," a mostly Russian and Ukrainian enclave inside Moldova, complete with a hammer and sickle on its flag, the ruble for its currency, and a strut that says it's still 1955. Russia, or rather, Transnistria, has threatened to secede if Moldova reunites with Romania, sparking a civil war. Truly, "a chip off the old block."

In the end, maybe the status quo is the best-of-the-bad solutions to the question of Moldova. Maybe a hung jury is what you want. Maybe "lose-lose" is as good as it gets. After all, a stalemate is a form of détente in one of the last unfinished battles of the Cold War. Neither side gets full custody. Both agree to "weekend visitations"—and to peaceful coexistence.

And, in a way, that's good for Moldova too, since it continues to get "support" from both parents.

So yet another child grows up without a true mother or father. Given what those parents are like, it's probably better off.

Chapter Eighteen

Land of the Lost

Haiti

Give a man a fish and you feed him for a day. Teach a man to fish, and he will sit in the boat and drink beer all day.
—Unknown

At first, I thought we were on the wrong flight. The plane was full, but few Haitians were on board.

Most of the other passengers were white, middle-class Southerners, moms and dads, and teenage daughters, dressed in colorful, matching t-shirts that made them look like they were on a field trip. In a way, they were, but this junket was not just for fun. Their t-shirts told you they were on a mission trip, going to build a church or paint a school.

More precisely, they were on a "Mission from God." And they were going to save Haiti. Just like all the other church groups that arrived in the country that day.

The weather was clear that morning. The plane took off and headed south toward the Caribbean. I loved saying "The Caribbean." We were moving to the Caribbean! Are there any more beautiful words in the English language?

I stared out the window the whole way. The sky and sea were reflections of each other. The sea also had cosmic blue blobs, here and there, like a summer snow cone. Tiny islands stuck their heads out of the water, basking in the sunlight.

The flight was a prelude to our tour in Haiti, I thought. Smooth and beautiful. After three years of revolution in Egypt, we were headed to its complete antithesis—a warm tropical island. Eager for a fresh start, I banished all the negative thoughts and images about Haiti. We would have a two-year vacation. All would be well.

About a half hour before landing, the sun disappeared, replaced by scattered clouds—first a few gray puffs, then larger and blacker. Soon the sky was dark, and the plane began to shake.

The mood changed suddenly and irrevocably.

I looked out the window and saw land below, pyramids of brown, barren mountains, sides stripped of every living thing. With the approaching storm, it looked like Dr. Frankenstein might live on the island.

My pulse quickened and my palms became slick. The worst images of what Haiti could be now flashed before my eyes. I had seen the movie *The Serpent and the Rainbow* too many times.

My wife and I wanted to live in the Caribbean for the same reasons people vacation there—warm sun, white sandy beaches, mountains, smiling faces, close to home. And we would have such niceties year-round.

But as the plane rattled and shook, I realized that we were not on vacation anymore and no longer in the Caribbean. We were approaching Haiti.

We were time-traveling again—this time, back to an almost-"Jurassic" world. The horror.

We landed in the capital, Port au Prince. The airport was nicer than I expected. I'm sure those arriving with kids were relieved by its appearance.

The relief didn't last long.

Chester was traveling with us, riding in the cargo section beneath the plane. I worried about whether he had survived the journey in one piece.

He was the last item off the plane, making a dramatic entrance to the country, as the handlers threw his box, with him inside, onto the baggage carousel. The box took a tumble and our poor dog rolled along inside, confused and shaken.

Going through customs, one of the "officials" tried to shake me down for a bogus "import fee" on the dog. "Such an amateur," I thought, as he stuttered the delivery of his attempted extortion. He had no idea who he was messing with.

We walked outside and looked for the driver to take us into town.

Although the interior is somewhat clean and organized, Port au Prince Airport is located in one of the worst parts of the capital. You have to run the gauntlet when you exit. There is no other way to get into the city.

And there is no buffer zone between the airport and Haitian reality, no gradual process of settling in and getting used to your new surroundings. It greets you right away when you get off the plane—Whoosh! You're in one of the scariest slums, in one of the poorest countries in the world.

There should be a sign that says, "Welcome to Haiti! It's not too late to go back to the airport."

The title, "Port au Prince," has become a gross—pun intended—exaggeration, perhaps even a sick joke. I'm convinced that its name is part of a disinformation campaign intended to trick would-be tourists into coming to the country.

The city has a port, all right, but there is nothing "royal" about the place. To me, its nickname "Port au Potty" was a more accurate description.

PaP begins at the water's edge and crawls up the nearby mountains. The higher up you go, the nicer the surroundings. The mountain tops are cooler and still have some trees. Most of the slums are down by the water. The rich live at the top. The poor, at the bottom. The airport is at the bottom.

Some say that if you want to see how the rest of the world lives, hop a flight to Africa. The sights and smells will give a healthy jolt to your reality and make you count your blessings.

But you don't have to go half-way around the world. Simply take the two hour flight south to the "Congo of the Caribbean," and you will enjoy the same effect.

The saddest part is that Haiti didn't have to turn out this way. The island was blessed with enormous potential. There are beautiful mountains, beaches, rich land for agriculture, plentiful rain, and warm sunshine. Indeed, there are a dozen islands in the same neighborhood that have made themselves relatively prosperous by using these natural resources. But throughout Haiti's history, no government managed the resources properly. No one planned for the future. Everything was done for short-term gain and greed.

Haiti is like the kid you sat next to in school who goofed off all day, didn't do his homework, and gave the future the finger. Now, in the grown-up world, he has no job, no skills, and still can't read—only about sixty percent of Haitians are literate, compared to ninety percent literacy in the remainder of Latin America and the Caribbean. And those who can are literate in a one-country language called Haitian Creole, which is basically what would happen if *The Little Rascals* hijacked French. They have words like *"pwojet"* and *"construksyon."*

He's also burned through all of his savings. As a result, Haiti resembles an animal carcass that's been picked clean. The locals have chopped down ninety-eight percent of the trees. They have over-fished the coasts, polluted the fresh water, and strip-mined the hills for rocks and minerals. Any large land animals were killed off long ago. The country is covered with garbage, including many of its beaches, the reality of which seemed especially wrong.

A calendar put out by a local bank was called "Haiti's Natural Heritage" and included pictures of domestic flora and fauna. In the pages, the best they could come up with were close-up photographs of a frog, a bird, and some flowers. They were beautiful flowers though.

Haiti is the capital of complacency. If Cairo makes you crazy, then Haiti makes you lazy. There you learn that even your brain can give in to the lazies.

There's no urgency to get anything done because tomorrow will also be warm. We can do it then. But, "Tomorrow," as the cliché goes, "never comes."

Infrastructure is nothing to write home about either. Or perhaps it is. Americans complain when the electricity goes out for a few hours or days after a bad storm.

But how would you like it if it went out every day? Like clock-work. EVERY SINGLE DAY. At virtually the same time. Indeed, the only reliable thing about Haitian power is its unreliability.

If this happened in the US, there would be outrage in the streets. In Haiti, it's expected.

The blackouts happen because the country doesn't have the capacity to run the power all the time, so they turn it off at about 6 am and turn it back on late in the evening. (That is, unless it starts to rain. For some reason, the electricity won't work in the rain.) Of course, these are the hours when you are awake and most productive. You know, when you do stuff and need electricity.

As a result, the well-to-do get generators and batteries, which can run lights and small appliances until the evening. But most of the country cannot afford these things and, therefore, go without power during the day.

Every time I went home to the US, I was amazed that there was electricity twenty-four hours a day—even when it was raining.

When you arrive in a new country, other expats want to get your impressions of the place. Sometimes, when asked what I thought about Haiti, I blurted out, "The name says it all!" "Haiti is a country in search of a disaster." "It's like the Congo opened a branch office in the Caribbean." "And the cities were designed by the same architects who brought you the South Bronx." "The country's a warm garbage dump covered in flowers." "There's a reason it wasn't called 'Lovie'." "People go to Haiti when Somalia just isn't dreadful enough."

Or, sometimes, I would just spit out, like someone with Tourette's syndrome, "Hate," "Heat," "Hades," "Hell." The words were so close to "Haiti," they slid right off my tongue.

You can make jokes like this to other expats in most countries. They're used, mostly, to blow off steam. But, for some reason, such an attitude was frowned upon in Haiti, even among foreigners. Sarcasm had no place in this country.

Because of this, living in Haiti felt like one long photo shoot—you always had to smile. For some reason, if you were not smiling, people immediately assumed you're angry.

Perhaps as a result, Haiti is also "The Land of Political Correctness." The "Disconnect Between Hope and Reality." "The Land of Grin and Bear It," not to mention "Hold Your Tongue and Bite Your Lip."

"At least it's warm," I told myself when gunfire rang out in the middle of the night, and our security guard lay half naked in the driveway next to an empty bottle of rum. Or pedestrians peed on the wall in front of our house. Or when Haitians literally barked at Chester when we went for a walk.

The things we put up with to be warm.

Fortunately for Haiti, the carpe diem kid, it receives an "allowance" from a new set of "parents"—international donors who can't bear to see him slowly implode.

And who can blame them? Who would fault anyone for trying to save someone from starving to death? Their intentions are, indeed, honorable.

But in the end, the assistance is just a form of life support. It keeps the country breathing but doesn't give it much hope for a bright future. After all, the donations were meant to be a short-term fix, not a permanent solution. That being said, few make significant progress while still on life support.

It has been argued, even by development specialists, that much of the Haitian assistance has been a gigantic waste, and that Haiti is the poster child for the failure of long-term, international aid.

Indeed, perhaps never before has such a small country received so much from so many people for such a long time. Armies of the best and brightest relief workers have journeyed to the Haitian shores for decades. Yellow school buses, donated by churches and communities in the States, prowl the city streets. Billions and billions of dollars have been spent.

What's the result of all this aid and assistance? Haiti is still the poorest country in the Western Hemisphere.

At least many relief workers make good salaries. I often thought the organizations should change their slogan to "Making liberal arts majors rich, one disaster at a time."

As an aside, you can observe other US donations at work in Haiti. For example, ever wonder what happens to those old t-shirts you donated to Goodwill? Some will make the twelve hundred mile journey to Port au Prince, where they're sold for a few bucks on the street—in this case, literally, on the street—since vendors display their goods for sale directly on the pavement. Locals choose the t-shirts based on their size and color, since most can't read the English inscriptions. I loved to look at them as they paraded through the city. I saw Kappa Delta sorority and high school prom shirts on local street toughs. Others were more snarky, like the "I'm right and you're wrong!" boldly worn by a schoolgirl. A friend swears he saw "I love dick!" on an old lady's shirt.

Haiti also has an image problem, a common trait in other parts of the world. For example, no matter how great the beaches, most people don't want to vacation in Liberia. And if there were ever a country in need of an image consultant, it's Haiti. It might as well be called "Mug Whitey Land," for all the connotations the mere name of the country suggests. Most have already made up their mind about the place before ever paying a visit. That's why they stay at home.

What do you think of when you hear the word "Haiti?" If you answered honestly, your response would probably consist of a strange combination of dictators, earthquakes, burning tires, machetes, and garbage.

Tell friends, family, strangers, even telephone operators—anyone, who's not a missionary—that you live and work in Haiti, and then sit back and enjoy the shock and sympathy. Normally, there is a long pause after the news. Then responses follow, such as, "Why!" which is an exclamation, not a question. Or, the apologetic, "I'm so sorry." And, finally, the searching for hope "When can you leave?" In this case, living in Haiti is seen as a punishment or a prison sentence.

So, if it were up to me, I would start a campaign to officially change the country's name to something like "The Republic of Free Hugs" or "The Land of a Thousand Suns." No, wait, that sounds too hot. You don't want to advertise that you'll blister there. How about just "The Kingdom of Cookies?"

Indeed, the local government has recently tried to market the country as a tourist destination. The problem is they're putting the cart before the horse. Most of the infrastructure—hotels, security, travel agencies, ground transportation, English-speakers—is not sufficient for an influx of tourists. Thus, if successful, this marketing ploy would just end up making an even larger number of people disappointed in the country.

As a result, a visit to Haiti is still rough and off-the-beaten path, euphemistically labeled "adventure tourism" by die-hard optimists.

One time, we visited Île-à-Vache, "Cow Island," a tiny and beautiful Haitian island off the southern coast. To get there from PaP, you must first drive to Les Cayes, one of Haiti's larger cities, and wait for the hotel to send a boat to pick you up. We were, unfortunately, the first people to ever do this, so no one could tell us when the boat would arrive. We showed up early and waited at a small, garbage-choked dock, watching little kids "play" with stray puppies by tossing them, head over heels, into the sea.

A few hours later, the boat arrived, and we made the six-mile trip past Haitians free-diving for conch. These divers foreshadowed things to come.

After about a half hour, we entered Abaka Bay, within spitting distance of the shore. Our beach vacation was right in front of us!

Then the boat conked out. We had it made it all that way—over the mountains and through the waves—only to be left bobbing a few hundred feet from the dock. We would've jumped in and swam the rest of the way if it weren't for our luggage. Eventually, another boat towed us to shore.

And it was a beautiful shore. The stretch of white powdery sand was virtually untouched except for a row of small cabanas fifty feet from the water. You wake up and dive right in. Little kids hide in nearby bushes, ready to jump out and act as guides for visitors exploring other parts of the island.

On the way back, the boat died, again, a few hundred feet from Les Cayes.

And that's Haitian tourism in a nutshell. While the potential is huge, you just can't seem to get there.

What's the solution then? What can be done to help Haiti?

I haven't a clue.

I do know what doesn't work.

All the money in the world won't make a country like Haiti prosperous, or even sustainable, at least in the long run. You can't help someone help themselves until they are ready. It won't take. And you will just end up emptying your pockets indefinitely.

Such unending support also prevents the Haitians from "growing up," since they never learn to take care of themselves.

The Haitians will tell you the same thing. For example, many admit openly that they are not "ready" for democracy and don't have the capacity to make informed decisions. As a result, Haitians glorify the "good old days" of the 1950s and 1960s under the former dictator, François Duvalier, aka "Papa Doc." Sure, he created a police state with a harsh regime, they say, but things worked. Whether it's more nostalgia than truth, they claim that the country was far more civilized and few went hungry when the government used a strong hand to tell the people what to do.

Sometimes, this carefree dysfunction even affected the friendly neighborhood US government officials stationed there.

One time, the *responsables* at Embassy Port au Prince decided that, as part of American Black History Month, the Haitian national employees in the building should be honored with re-enactments from the American Civil Rights movement. Other than being black, most Haitians have no knowledge of, or attachment to, any US Civil Rights movements. But the American bigwigs were excited, so the Rosa Parks story was chosen. Have I mentioned that most Haitians have no idea who Rosa Parks was?

A pretend "bus" was built out of office chairs in an embassy atrium. The real problem occurred after the cleanup—or lack thereof. Though workers took away the chairs, they left up several provocative signs for days afterward. The signs had been hung to portray the racial context of the recreated Rosa Parks incident. So, in the middle of the US embassy, a building where most of the employees are black Haitians, hung slogans like "Whites Only" and "Colored Section." Seriously? Welcome to the world of "we'll take care of it later."

Eventually, the same careless (or was it now carefree?) mindset spread to yours truly as well. (Indeed, perhaps the transformation taught me the difference between being carefree and careless. Only in the Caribbean can you be poor and still carefree.)

I learned to jettison many of my cares, and after refusing to heed any common sense, I learned to love my new home.

It wasn't an immediate process. But I don't think anyone can fall in love at first sight with Haiti.

One warm day folded into the next until I was able to look beyond some of the absurdity.

Much of my transformation happened after I escaped Port au Prince. By traveling outside of the capital, you realize that rural Haiti is a shockingly raw, magical, even Wizard-of-Oz-type land-scape where you expect the trees to come to life and scoop you up.

The mountains, green and brown and shrouded in fog, resemble Central Africa. Farmers build Asian-style terraced staircases to squeeze a few more plants on each hillside. Mountains are capped with a single line of pine trees like exclamation points.

There are even some beautiful, trash-free, beaches, like Île-à-Vache, with sugary sand that slides into crystal-clear, swimming pool water.

The weather also changed me. I used to think that real life re-quired that you had to be cold, at least part of the time. A Catholic, Midwest upbringing taught me that winter was penance for having enjoyed a warm summer. After all, there were consequences for everything, "equal and opposite reactions," if you will. But Haiti proved that you can be warm all year and still guilt-free.

All this being said, I think my favorite part of Haiti was the drivers. Perhaps I was easily impressed since I was coming from Egypt, but man, I learned to admire Haitians drivers. Their demean-or makes Port au Prince nothing like Cairo.

If the cliché that you can judge a country by the way they drive is true, then Haitians are absolute saints. Most function like they are taking their first driver's test—slow, almost, painfully slow. They practically drive in slow-motion. It's like their cars don't go above twenty miles per hour, which is actually not too far from the truth.

They are considerate and non-aggressive, almost absurdly so. In fact, they probably cause more accidents by being so considerate.

Haitians prove that traffic lights are over-rated and largely un-necessary. Even in the capital, you can easily count the number of signals. In fact, most Port au Prince intersections do without them. Yet somehow, everything works fine. Cars slow down as they ap-proach. Generally, the one to get there first gets to go through. And, if there is traffic on all sides, each takes her turn. When one side has had the right of way for a while, the others start to get restless by inching forward and eventually the moving side backs down. I saw only a small number of car accidents in two years in Haiti.

For Haitians, driving is, ironically, a passive activity. Unlike Americans, they are not territorial about the road. It's not yours or theirs. It's just a road, and everyone gets to use it.

It doesn't matter how bad the traffic is, Haitians will usually make room for you to pull onto a busy road in front of them. You give them a friendly honk in return to say "Thanks." And they'll honk back, a friendly "You're welcome."

Most of them, anyway. There are the five or ten percenters, the troublemakers, who drive like they own the road, or are in such a hurry, they can't follow the unspoken Haitian rules of the road. They've probably lived in other countries and seen how they drive. Still, the Haitians understand and let them be this way. Hakuna Matata.

As a result, it is perfectly acceptable for someone stuck in traffic to drive down the wrong side of the road, or even on a sidewalk, skip the big line, and cut back in front of everyone else. Mean-while, others continue to wait hours for the line to budge.

And what happens after this daredevil maneuver?

In Haiti? Nothing. Crickets. Not a single honk. No fists, yells, or fingers.

In Haiti, few seem to care about things they can't control. Or about anything, really. If Egyptians are often fussy and overbearing, Haitians are their complete opposites.

It was in moments like this that I realized how much time and energy I had wasted in my life worrying about things that were beyond my control. I wanted the zen-like inner peace, or perhaps just the indifference, to rub off on me. In time, I grew to accept, and even enjoy, Haiti's complacency and laid-back shabbiness.

Maybe the rest of the world is too serious, too concerned with appearances, cleanliness, and order, I thought. Maybe uninterrupted electricity is over-rated. Maybe it is okay to pee in the street as others walk by.

Why waste your time worrying about everything? Who cares? It's warm outside. Have another drink. Everything will be fine. And, if it isn't, there's always tomorrow.

On a deeper level, I think everyone, at some point, longs to return to childhood, to a time when there were few responsibilities, little competition, no concerns about jobs or money. A place like Haiti can take you back to this time. The whole country seems to be built on this philosophy. And perhaps as a result, Haiti is one of the few places I'd like to return to and live once again.

In the end, I think I will remember the weather in Haiti the most. After all, I didn't really accomplish much more than just enjoying the sunshine, tracing the footsteps of all the other expats who came before me. And I wasn't proud of anything in particular, except perhaps that, over the course of two years, I never once—outside of work—wore long pants, long sleeves, closed-toed shoes, or even a jacket. Yeah, that's pretty cool, actually.

Maybe that's the real lesson of Haiti. That there are no lessons— or just too many of them. So we overthink and overanalyze every- thing, when most days we should just pee where we want and not worry about tomorrow. Just make sure you breathe through your mouth.

Chapter Nineteen

Unhappy Drunks

England

> It is most absurdly said, in popular language, of any man, that he
> is disguised in liquor; for, on the contrary, most men are dis-
> guised by sobriety.
> —Thomas de Quincy, *Confessions of an English Opium-Eater*

You can tell a lot about a country by how they drink. And why they
drink. For example, do they drink to get drunk? What happens to
them when they get drunk? Are they happy or sad drunks?

Stereotypically, the French drink to feel romantic. Italians drink
to see beauty. Americans drink to feel good. The Russians drink to
remember. The Japanese drink to forget.

And the English drink to get drunk. Do they have to be over-
achievers in everything?

That, and then they want to fight.

When I lived there, there was no such thing as just going out for
a beer. You went out to get "piiissssed!" Stumbling, mumbling,
mind-erasing, vomit-soaked, incarceratedly obliterated. It was the
main objective of the night, almost a suicidal quest to destroy yourself. If you came home sober or even just mildly buzzed, you

missed your target. You were shunned like a kamikaze pilot who's returned safely to base.

Curiously, the English are considerate enough to announce to everyone around them when they were about to hop on the booze train . . . "I do believe I'm getting pissed."

Perhaps they were polite up to that point because they knew everything was about to change.

Booze was their ticket to exit civilization and return to their own "dark age." To take off their mask and muzzle and become a different person. Or maybe return to the one buried deep inside.

And they wanted to make it official with a formal announcement, so they could say and do whatever the hell they wanted and not be held accountable for any of it. After all, they warned you!

Of course, the obvious question to the amateur anthropologist is "Why?" What makes them want, or even need, to get drunk, so very drunk? Why is it necessary to assume an alternate identity every time? And why is fighting the only thing so many want to do after that?

To answer that, we have to look at the grander question of civilization.

Our world, as we know it, largely exists because of the English. Darwin, Newton and Milton, Hobbes and Shakespeare, Locke, Mills and Keynes. People like these created or codified many of the profound ideas that make up the bedrock of modern civilization. Their work represents one of the largest canons on how to live a life and govern a country. The legal, social, scientific, political, and economic frameworks and foundations that make our lives possible often trace their roots to the land of Stonehenge.

And clearly the ideas have been extremely successful.

Look around at how many countries have actually contributed to civilization, let alone dominated the field? Sure, you can name a few well-known people from this or that country. But what other nation has given so much to humanity?

In a world of irresponsible children, the English are often the only "adults in the room."

And look what happened when they produced their own "offspring"—the "Baby Englands," if you will—countries which were settled and developed by their pioneers, such as America, Canada, Australia, and New Zealand. It's not a coincidence that they're the most prosperous nations in history. The places where everyone else wants to live.

Of course, the English have made mistakes. Even enormous ones. But they've given the world far more than they've taken from it. And, unlike most empires in history, England usually left its colonies far better off than they found them, introducing them to a level of modern life that likely would have escaped the locals even today.

The English didn't invent democracy or capitalism. It's been an evolutionary process. Maybe they simply added to the ideas and improved on them. Or maybe they just codified what's been floating around in the air, in our DNA.

Whatever the case, they influenced major ideas and vice versa. The ideas, eventually, became part of England's personality. The people began to take them around everywhere.

And you can see them on more practical levels. For example, the English are famous for concepts like their love of fair play and waiting in line.

But let's take a closer look.

Many think the English love to queue. But they don't, really, love to queue. Nobody likes to wait. They love the queue. That it exists. That, even in the "wilderness" of a shopping mall or busy airport, there is some sort of rule, order, even civilization—there's that word again—and fair play. The queue translates to "Whoever got here first, deserves to be first." Pure and simple.

The line is also a microcosm of society. How it is organized reflects how things work, or don't, in your country. And to the

English, society today, with some exceptions, should be a level playing field. Everyone knows the pre-determined rules and is free to act accordingly. And, if you wait your turn, you'll eventually be taken care of, as will everyone else.

The line is also about personal initiative, which is an essential component to this political and economic philosophy. If you want to get up early in the morning and wait in line, you can be "ahead"—literally and metaphorically—of others. As in capitalism, your personal enterprise is, in theory anyway, directly proportional to what you receive in life. Obviously, America too has thrived on these principles.

This concept seems simple, but it's not so obvious to other countries.

In the Third World, for example, a line is a line in name only. And not even completely in name. To call them "lines" is a misnomer. There are no lines in the Third World. There are clusters or half-circles.

In these countries, the only rule is "There are no rules." Or "The mob rules." And the only law is from the jungle. It's every savage for himself.

This is how it works, Third World style. Everyone huddles around a window, for example, waiting, hoping, desperate to make eye contact with the person behind the counter. People try to cut in from all sides, squeezing, groaning, throwing elbows and dirty looks. They're like a herd of cows pushing toward the feed trough. A few inches can be valuable territory.

Why do they act like this? Who knows? It's probably rooted in some kind of panic that goes along with waiting in a place with severely limited resources. You fear that the toilet paper will run out before your turn, that all the seats will be taken before you board. The notion of fair play hasn't arrived here yet. So you're compelled to rush forward and crowd around the window, like some UN official is throwing out the last of the high protein biscuits. It's a primal, unconscious action. You just feel your feet moving toward the life source.

You'd cluster too if in this situation. If you didn't, if you stood behind the guy in front of you, tried to make some kind of rudimentary formation, you'd, literally, wait forever. Someone would continuously step in front of you from the side, and you'd still be standing there today, reading this book from the same place in line. You see, the person behind the counter cannot be counted on to demand or enforce any semblance of order. She doesn't care a whit about fair play or who gets served next. To her, a level playing field is only good for soccer. It's a free-for-all in here, because it's a free-for-all out there. And so, in the Third World, the cluster, too, is a microcosm of society.

So England is a role-model for civility and fair play. Of course, in some ways, its people probably overthink these concepts. Too much of a good thing can be bad, after all. And, in England's case, society becomes too controlling and overbearing. Because no one can act civilized all the time. Everyone needs to express themselves and blow off steam now and then, to say and do what they want, rather than merely what is appropriate.

So the English drink to get drunk. They get pissed, because they're so—pissed.

As a result, drinking is often a desperate activity. Many countries could probably exist without alcohol, but I don't think England is one of them.

And they're not happy drunks, slapping you on the back, telling you how much they love you.

The English tell you how much they want to kick your ass. Booze turns every English lad into Mike Tyson.

They fight because they're angry at everyone who tries to control them when they're sober. And when they're drunk, this means everyone around them. Inebriation is payback time.

As the saying goes, "It's hard to be a clown when you have to run the circus." To the English, time spent drinking means time to let go. To hand over the reins for a few hours.

So forgive the English these transgressions. There are far worse sins. After all, you probably owe your current condition to them. Their countrymen (and women) have contributed more to our quality of life and civilization than any other country.

So the next time you see a drunk Englishman, buy him a round. After all, he's probably earned it. He'll still want to hit you, though, so better not ask him about his favorite soccer team.

Chapter Twenty

Going Back to See the Elephants

Bulgaria Redux

You never depart from us, but yet, only with difficulties do we
return to You.
—St. Augustine, *Confessions*

"You can't go back to see the elephants." You hear this expression
all the time on safari. It means that, after seeing an especially beautiful animal, many decide to return later to the same spot, hoping to
relive the moment. But, at that point, the animal has gone. The
lesson? Remember the fleeting experience, for it was meant to
happen only once.

When it comes to Bulgaria, I ignore this lesson repeatedly, returning to the country almost annually since the mid-1990s. While
most of the elephants are, indeed, long gone, just being in the same
place helps me remember what they were like. They were huge.
And sometimes loud and smelly.

It's striking how much and how little has changed in Bulgaria
since then. As noted, the country has joined the EU and NATO and
become, on paper anyway, a full-blown democracy with a free
market economy. There is enormous foreign investment, new shops

and restaurants. Bulgarians now have the freedom to travel, live, and work in any other EU country.

I can't help but feel that Bulgaria joined Europe too late, however. It's like they arrived at the party at 2 am, just as it was wrapping up.

Europe is tired. Its best days are behind it. The party's over.

I've had this feeling a lot in recent years. I once visited the Acropolis during a layover in Athens. It was 2009, the heart of the financial crisis. The day was ending, and I was headed back to the airport, so I flagged down a taxi. The trip would cost close to fifty dollars, and yet the driver looked at his watch and thought about the request. "Mmm . . . No, can't do it. It's almost dinner time. Gotta get home!"

As he drove away, I said without thinking, and to no one in particular, "And that's why you're poor. You just traded a good fare for an on-time meal." Europe's old and set in her ways. She won't bend anymore, even to make an extra buck.

The next taxi driver was Pakistani. He didn't have a problem taking me wherever I wanted to go.

But Europe's not alone. Bulgaria too is no longer herself.

She has traded culture for investment. Many parts now look and feel like the rest of the continent. There are Walmart-style hyper-markets, drive-thru McDonalds, banking by phone, even Western-style subdivisions. The streets are clogged with imported cars. The country is hopped up on a wave of consumer goods, trying to make up for years of communist deprivation.

It very well may have been a "deal with the devil." In the process of modernization, Bulgaria has lost much of her identity. The country has become a corporate franchise run out of headquarters in Brussels—a far cry from the "mom-and-pop" corner store of the past. Perhaps history has finally ended in Bulgaria.

But that's just one side of things. On the other side, I'm glad for some of the smaller changes. For example, maybe Bulgarians will finally stop using ketchup for tomato sauce on pizza. And the adult in me says that everyone must grow up eventually. No one can live like a teenager forever and be happy. So I don't blame them because I'd probably do the same thing. After all, using newsprint for toilet paper gets old.

But my impetuous side says that Bulgaria was most charming when it was Bulgarian, even if that meant it was ugly, hard, or confused at times. At least it wasn't pre-packaged or "sanitized for your protection." What you saw around you and in others was largely organic, both literally and figuratively. Their pride, personality, and traditions hadn't been imported or faked.

Bulgaria was the perfect "starter country" for an expat. It was a happy medium between the post-modern, over-developed First World of, say, Western Europe, and the harsher Third World of West Africa or South Asia. Bulgaria was still raw and rough, edgy and unpredictable, without leaving you at risk for terrorism or leprosy. Even when the shops were almost empty and there was no hot water, you would still survive. No one was dying in the streets. And there were plenty of joys to be had in the country.

These days, Bulgarians are also unsure whether the last few years have been a fair deal. Many are nostalgic for the "good old days," even if, as always, they probably weren't as good as they remember.

This is nothing new—no pun intended—as nostalgia is another major commodity of the Balkans. The people don't like change, especially rapid change, which is all they've gotten in recent years. Ironically, the majority don't think that EU membership has made their lives better. This sentiment prevails, even while it is clear that they enjoy many benefits with these changes. It seems they want a heaping serving of their old ways with a side of prosperity.

The Balkans are full of such contradictions. In Sofia, my first little old landlady was a staunch nationalist. She wasn't crazy about the minorities in the country—Turks, Jews, and especially Gypsies.

I found it strange, then, that she hung a picture on her wall of a young Gypsy girl in full costume. I once pointed to the picture and expressed my confusion. "Yes," she responded with a smile. "She is beautiful."

In reality, both Bulgaria and I have grown up, apart, and, mostly, moved on. We cannot go back to the simpler chapters of our lives and are doing what's best for us. As a friend used to say, most American expats eventually look for someone who knows what *The Brady Bunch* is. Maybe that's for the better. Along this path to adulthood, though, there's been much kicking and screaming. And we both keep one eye looking backward.

Years after leaving Bulgaria, I took my wife to Sofia for her first visit. Upon arrival, the country seemed happy to see me again. But it was not so sure about my new "guest," shrouding itself in fog the entire visit—in essence refusing my wife the chance to get a good look at anything.

But a part of Bulgaria, in my mind, will never change. It will always be my escape plan, my Plan B, my do-over. The blank slate where I can reinvent myself if need be. And it will always be my "band"—as in *The Blues Brothers'* Jake Blues yelling in church, "The band, the band!" upon discovering the path along which he can start over.

"Bulgaria . . . Bulgaria!" The country's air of freedom and mystery still stirs my insides when I hear its name. I feel sorry for those who've never had such a feeling.

Each time I return to Sofia, I visit Svetlana, a long-time friend who believes that the old ways are still the best. Talking to her, I experience an instant reality check, if reality is one of the stages of grief. Svetla sees only the worst in everything that has happened in Bulgaria since the end of communism. None of the changes have been positive. She is the "Debbie Downer" of Bulgaria, putting an end to any excitement you felt upon your return.

During my last visit, we discussed the economic changes. "Oh, they're terrible," Svetla remarked. "There are no good jobs. The foreigners buy up everything. These new supermarkets are putting the little shops out of business. They can't compete."

At the end of the evening, Svetla walked me to the main street to catch a taxi. She and her husband planned to do some shopping at a nearby store. "You going over there?" I asked, pointing at the new Austrian supermarket. "Oh yes," Svetla said, eyes lighting up. "It's incredible—they have everything!"

Postscript:
Clean and Happy People

America

Sweet is the remembrance of troubles when you are in safety.
—Euripides, *Andromeda*

"Welcome home," says the passport officer. You smile and breathe deeply. Maybe your eyes even water a little. After all, it's more than just a greeting, it's like a secret password into an exclusive club. Have any sweeter words ever been spoken?

It doesn't matter if she's sincere. Delivering that line is the most important part of her job. Those simple, even cliché, words are immensely powerful and evocative. The whole scene feels like a Hallmark commercial.

You stepped off the plane in Chicago, Atlanta, or Washington, DC. You made it home again, across enemy lines, back to home base. Safe. Home. Even the passport officer said so.

Whenever I land in the US, I feel like the Pope. I want to drop to my knees and kiss the ground after stepping off the plane.

I want to see someone in overalls. I want to hear a Southern accent.

151

The return should be dramatic. After all, you passed the test, won the game, survived the goofy, stinky, weird foreigners who taught you so much about themselves, their countries, the world, human nature, and, lest we forget, yourself. But perhaps the biggest thing they taught you is how great your own country is.

All the madness of the past weeks and months is now gone, wiped away in an instant.

You look around, and suddenly, everything is different—the faces, the clothes, the manners, the order, the tidiness. It's all so familiar and comforting. Everything feels shiny and new. You want to take it all inside. Time begins again, giving you a fresh start in "The Land of Clean and Happy People."

And if you don't feel this way, you probably didn't see or learn enough overseas. Perhaps you took few chances, rarely strayed from your comfort zone.

Returning to the US should feel like, when you were a kid, slamming the screen door after a long day of playing in the mud, taking a hot shower, slipping into clean pajamas, and savoring a nice meal.

Why? Because the US is the richest, fairest, safest, most powerful country in history.

Is it perfect? Is it paradise? Of course not. But it's much easier to appreciate its greatness when it's held up to other countries.

Each time I return home, especially from the Third World, I see the best in America. And for me, the best part is a small town, the complete antithesis to a place like Egypt. Overnight, I can go from a city of twenty million to one of twenty thousand. A town where strangers greet each other. A place so clean you can eat off the sidewalks. And where the only honking comes from the ducks in the park.

Being here makes me want to engage in "ancestor worship." I want to sink to my knees every day, thanking the family members who came before me. Those who had the courage to get on a boat and cross the cold, dark ocean hundreds of years ago for a better life. A life they passed on to generations. I am immensely grateful to them, because I've seen how the other half around the world lives. I realize how different things could have been. So I'm relieved they chose to get on that boat. And, I like to think, they passed on some of that pioneer blood to me.

In my mind, most of the hard work in the US was done by our ancestors, long before we were born. By those wielding muskets and rifles in the Revolutionary and the Civil Wars. By a group of wise men who established the legal framework to make us a great nation.

Of course, much has changed since those days, for better and for worse.

The better keeps me coming back to the US. The worse makes me want to leave again soon.

We may not be as free as we were in the past. But we do have more options than any other place in the world. Food, drink, music, movies, books, academia, architecture, nature, climate. You can find virtually anything here, from hot to cold, high to low brow, mountains to valleys, Columbia to community college—almost anything you could possibly want is out there somewhere.

Some believe that if you enjoy living overseas, you must hate your country. For me, nothing is further from the truth.

I will always be a red-blooded American. Not one who bad-mouths his country, while traveling abroad. And not some kind of "halfsy" or hyphenated adjective. One team is enough for me. My home's given me everything, and I should return the favor.

I love being an American—a runt and a grunt. We are the toughest out there. Why? Because we don't bring many pretensions or expectations to a fight. We don't care about obscure things like background or pedigree. We study results and how to achieve them.

I also love what critics call our "provincialism." We are largely an insular, self-made entity. I actually love that most Americans don't have a passport, can't speak another language, think that France is in London. And best of all? They don't care. After all, I do enjoy living overseas, but I don't bring much of it back home with me. I want to knock my boots off when I come through the door.

And so I love America. I just don't want to live here—long-term, anyway.

Because each time I return home, I also feel like Gilligan when he builds a pair of wings to fly off the island. Despite breaking several laws of physics, they work, and he manages to get up pretty high in the air. But when he's reminded that he can't fly, he begins to doubt himself and promptly plummets to the ground.

The US is no country for young men. Most of the good ideas, maybe even the idea of having ideas, have dissipated in recent years. Or maybe, as they say, it all started to go downhill when the frontier closed.

The beats, the hippies, the commies, the cowboys, the punks, the rebels, the real artists, all the people who lived for something different, something more immaterial—where did they all go?

The US is now like a giant retirement home. A place where no one takes risks anymore. Where most—even the young—are set in their ways, craving only safety and comfort. Such obsessions dictate a life that must be up-front and predictable at all the times. There's no room for nuance, subtlety, or sarcasm. Hell, becoming overly sensitive is now a national past-time.

We move less as a country. It's "The Age of Extreme Individualism." And yet, we remain in the middle, perched on a narrow path, afraid to stray too far from the crowd.

Take a walk through a modern college campus. Most of the students now look and dress the same. For them, there's no time for exploring the world or trying new things. Their studies are merely a bullet point on a resume, an element of their "training" on the path to landing a good job and money. Perhaps a few still lay on the grass, contemplating grand ideas. But the majority of students march from class to class, heads down, eyes locked on cell phone screens, thumbs pressed against the refresh button, oblivious to much of what goes on around them. Solitary. Safe. And these are the young ones?

For me, the frontier was reopened in other countries.

That's what's special about living overseas. Every day is brand new and full of possibilities—to learn something new, to see and do unusual things. You can't predict what will happen at any given moment. Every day, you also have the chance to meet someone new. And I don't mean someone you didn't know before, but someone who is actually different from you, with thoughts and experiences that are truly foreign. Such a life is stimulating and addictive, like a daily adrenaline rush.

Being overseas also equals anonymity. At home, you live in the shadow of your culture. It surrounds you and influences your actions. But when you're away from it, your true self emerges. You develop a stronger identity and are freer to choose who you want to be.

In the end, living in the US is like living with your parents. You love them very much, but let's be honest, you shouldn't stay with them after you've grown up, at least not for long.

Because after you've had a hot shower and a nice meal, you should be ready to go play in the mud again.

Acknowledgments

This book would have never happened without the love and support of my father and late mother, Charles and Carol Millick. They gave me a peaceful home in which to write and, perhaps most important, the upbringing and education that made me who I am. I am grateful to my wife, Britton, and mother-in-law, Ellen, for their love and encouragement. Both cheered me on from day one and made sure I stayed with the project until the end. I would also like to thank Michael Palmer and the good folks at *Arcadia Magazine*, who published my first essay. Michael went out of his way to find value in "Friendly Fire," after others had rejected the story. Special appreciation also goes to Hamilton Books and their outstanding team, especially Holly Buchanan, Bethany Davis, and Beverly Shellem, and to Meghan Voss at Utah State for her invaluable editing. Lastly, I want to personally thank all the extraordinary people I've met, in all the far-off countries, over the last twenty years. Despite my sarcasm and satire, I loved being with you and learning about your worlds. You gave me a grand life and asked for so little in return. I owe you everything.

About the Author

Todd Millick spent his career in the United States government. He studied medieval history at the University of Colorado and received a master's degree from Cambridge. He was also a Fulbright Scholar in Bulgaria. The chapter "Friendly Fire" was originally published in *Arcadia Magazine*, where it was nominated for the *Pushcart Prize*. Mr. Millick has also published a collection of poems called *Short and Sweet* (Middle Island Press, 2016). He lives somewhere around the world with his wife and dog.

www.ingramcontent.com/pod-product-compliance
Lightning Source LLC
Chambersburg PA
CBHW030652270326
41929CB00007B/332